Religion in New Jersey Life Before the Civil War

Religion in New Jersey Life Before the Civil War

Edited by Mary R. Murrin

Papers Presented At The Fourteenth
Annual New Jersey History Symposium

December 4, 1982

TRENTON
1985
NEW JERSEY HISTORICAL COMMISSION, DEPARTMENT OF STATE

$6.50

For copies, write to the
New Jersey Historical Commission
Department of State
113 West State Street, CN 305
Trenton, NJ 08625

Thomas H. Kean, Governor
Jane Burgio, Secretary of State

Printed in the United States of America

Designed by Nancy H. Dallaire

ILLUSTRATIONS

Cover: View of the Presbyterian Church at Bloomfield. From John W. Barber and Henry Howe, *Historical Collections of the State of New Jersey* (New York, 1844).

LIBRARY OF CONGRESS CATALOGING IN PUBLICATION DATA

New Jersey History Symposium (14th : 1982 : Trenton, N.J.)
Religion in New Jersey Life Before the Civil War.

Bibliography: p.
1. New Jersey—Church history—Congresses. I. Murrin, Mary R. II. New Jersey Historical Commission. III. Title.
BR555.N5N48 1982 277.49 84-29483
ISBN 0-89743-062-X

Contents

Introduction

Most of the dynamic features of early American religion are nicely illustrated in New Jersey. From the founding of the colony to the early nineteenth century, the period covered by these four papers, New Jersey offered fertile ground for religious movements and revivals. Strikingly pluralistic, New Jersey had no established church, though its citizens and the rest of the Protestant world shared certain attitudes toward society and government.

What was New Jersey's denominational portrait in pre–Civil War New Jersey?[1] By the first Great Awakening, the colony had taken in several denominations, among them Anglicans, Baptists, Congregationalists, Dutch and German Reformed, Lutherans, Presbyterians and Quakers. From 1730 to 1850, as indicated on table 1, church growth and denominational strength appear to follow two definite patterns. First, the numbers of churches or congregations increase during the First and Second Great Awakenings (ca. 1730–40, ca. 1800–30) and decrease in the period following the Revolution. Second, the evangelical churches show the most impressive growth in the nineteenth century.

Although the earliest Quaker monthly meeting was established in 1672 in the East Jersey town of Shrewsbury, most Quakers settled in West Jersey. Salem Monthly Meeting was established in 1676, followed by Burlington in 1678. In 1745 Quakers or reputed Quakers represented substantial portions of the white populations of three counties in what had been West Jersey—Salem (16%), Gloucester (43%), and Burlington (51%)—and one in what had been East Jersey—Monmouth (41%). By 1730 there were twenty-four Quaker meetinghouses throughout New Jersey. The number of Quaker meetings continued to grow until the period around the Revolution. By 1832 there is again evidence of some growth, but the trend is reversed by 1850.

Presbyterians clustered in the Raritan Valley, Hopewell, Maidenhead, the Freehold area, and northern New Jersey. English Congregationalists fleeing the laxity of New England took refuge in Newark, Elizabethtown, Perth Amboy and Woodbridge. By the 1720s most of these had become Presbyterians, in a leap less of faith than of polity. For our purposes the two denominations are grouped together. Scottish Presbyterians and the Scots-Irish fleeing Stuart persecution settled in Freehold and throughout Monmouth county. Between 1730 and 1850 the number of Presbyterian churches increased dramatically, except for a sharp drop during the immediate post-Revolutionary period.

The Dutch Reformed clustered in Bergen, northern Essex, northern Morris, Somerset and Middlesex counties. Although they were among the first Europeans to settle in New Jersey (in Bergen in 1660), they established their first church twenty years later (in Hackensack in 1680) and only achieved prominence as a religious group after 1720 with the arrival of Theodorus Frelinghuysen. Their churches increased in number throughout the period from 1730 to 1850.

Anglican churches were located near the Delaware in Amwell, Hopewell, Trenton, Burlington, Greenwich and Maurice River, and on the other side of the colony in Middletown, Shrewsbury, Perth Amboy, Elizabethtown and around New Brunswick. Their number nearly doubled between 1730 and 1750 but decreased following the Revolution. The Anglican or Episcopal church declined in strength between 1775 and 1800, both as a part of the general church pattern and because Anglicans were usually Tories. Episcopalians did rebound in the nineteenth century; their churches doubled in number between 1800 and 1850.

Although there were Baptist churches established in Middletown in 1688 and Piscataway in 1689, New Jersey had few Baptists in the early

TABLE 1

CONGREGATIONS BY DENOMINATION

	1730	1750	1775	1800	1832	1850
Anglican or Episcopal	15	19	29	25	33	52
Baptist	6	12	30	30	61	108
Dutch or German Reformed	20	28	34	37	47	66
Lutheran[a]	8	14	18	(13)	(9)	7
Methodist[b]			9	20	(128)	312
Moravian		15	2	1		
Presbyterian/ Congregational[c]	23	52	81	50	85	157
Quaker	24	38	41	40	67	52
Roman Catholic		1	3			22
Other					10	
Total	96	179	247	216	440	776

[a]Figures for the number of Lutheran churches in 1800 and 1832 have been estimated on the basis of the rate of decline from 1775 to 1850.

[b]Gordon, in the *Gazetteer*, gives a figure for 1832 of 64 ministers and estimates two churches per minister.

[c]Presbyterians and Congregationalists have been combined. There were few differences in doctrine, and New Englanders who moved to New Jersey early in the eighteenth century generally shifted to the Presbyterian form of organization, primarily for political reasons.

colonial period. Most were scattered throughout central and northern New Jersey, with a few in the Cohansey area of what is now Cumberland County. However, the six churches established by 1730 had doubled in number by 1750 and more than redoubled by 1775. The table shows the usual plateau between 1775 and 1800, followed by dramatic growth between 1800 and 1850.

Lutheran churches clustered in northern Bergen, the Raritan Valley and Hunterdon County. Never very numerous, they increased only until 1775; thereafter their numbers declined sharply.

Until the Revolution, Methodists were a movement within the Anglican church rather than an independent church. They had very few churches in 1775. Most of their leaders, like those of the Anglicans, were Tories; both groups were adversely affected by the Revolution. For a variety of reasons Methodists were faster to regroup. Their church showed particular strength in the southern part of the state. They were the only denomination to grow significantly after the Revolution, doubling between 1775 and 1800. By 1850 they had become the largest denomination in the state.

The Methodists were among the evangelical sects, which grew impressively in New Jersey after the Second Awakening (see figure 1). For our purposes the term *evangelical* includes Baptists, Presbyterians, and Dutch Reformed as well as Methodists. Moravians are also classed as evangelical, but no information on that sect after 1800 is obtainable. All of these denominations included liturgical parties, but on the whole they should be placed in the evangelical camp. The evangelical churches experienced their most dramatic growth between 1832, when there were 321 of them, and 1850, when there were 643. Of the figures on table 1 the number for the Methodist churches is the most speculative.[2]

Information on the nonevangelical denominations in 1832 is incomplete. Only the Episcopalians showed growth—from thirty-three churches in 1832 to fifty-two in 1850. The number of Quaker meetings dropped precipitously between 1832 and 1850. The number of Lutheran churches in 1850 is estimated at nine, on the basis of the overall rate of decrease from 1775 to 1850. New Jersey counted 111 churches or meetings (Episcopalian, Lutheran, Quaker) in 1850. There were also twenty-two Catholic churches, a number which reflects the beginnings of Catholic immigration.

The evidence from New Jersey lends support to the theory that the Revolutionary generation marked the nadir of religious interest and provides evidence of the religious ferment of the Awakenings before and after the Revolution. The annual rates of growth of population and churches are quite close from 1730 to 1750 (see table 2). After 1750 they diverge markedly. Expressed somewhat differently, from 1730 to 1750 there was about one church to every 400 people. By 1775 that ratio had dropped to one to 524, and by 1800 it was one to nearly 1000. Thereafter, the ratio steadily improved, but as late as 1850 it was still lower than the level of 1730–1750. Obviously these ratios are only suggestive—one can hardly assume that all of these people went to church between 1730 and 1850. What both the church/population ratios and the figures for annual rates of growth suggest is that there was a crisis of religiosity between 1775 and 1800.

To look at these trends in greater detail, the annual rate of population growth slowed steadily from 1730 to 1830 and then increased rapidly

FIGURE 1

APPROXIMATE PERCENTAGE EVANGELICAL IN TOTAL CHURCH POPULATION

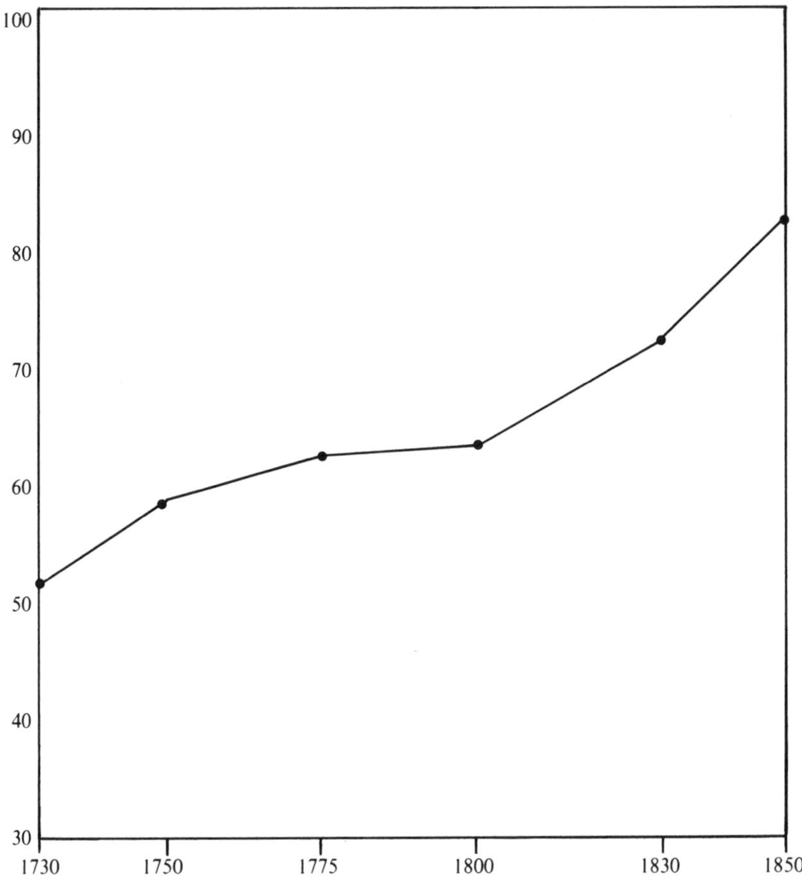

TABLE 2

CHURCH AND POPULATION GROWTH

	Population (to Nearest 100)	Growth Rate (%)[a]	Churches	Growth Rate (%)[a]	Population Per Church
1730	37,500		96		391
1750	71,400	3.3	179	3.2	399
1775[b]	129,500	2.5	247	1.3	524
1800	211,000	2.0	216	-.5	977
1832[b]	330,800	1.4	440	2.2	752
1850	490,000	2.2	776	3.2	631
1775–1832		1.7		1.0	

[a]Average per year during period since previous figure.
[b]Population figures are extrapolated from census figures for 1772 and 1830.

to 1850. The annual rate of church growth also fell off from 1730 to 1800, but much more dramatically. From 1730 to 1750 it nearly kept pace with population growth, reflecting the intense religious activity of the First Great Awakening. The rate of church growth slowed noticeably from 1750 to 1775, and then dropped precipitously; it was negative from 1775 to 1800. While the figures for 1800 are quite sketchy, this negative rate supports the argument that the Revolutionary generation put less energy into religion. Growth then picked up dramatically from 1800 to 1832—around the time of the Second Great Awakening. From 1832 to 1850 the annual rate of growth for churches was greater even than for the population.

MILTON J COALTER and Martha Blauvelt together follow New Jersey Presbyterians from the 1730s to the 1830s. Coalter's paper is an intellectual biography of the First Awakening itinerant pastor from New Brunswick, Gilbert Tennent. Blauvelt analyzes the change in the structure of revivals from the First to the Second Awakening. Both essays discuss the effect of the revival phenomenon on the church and its followers.

Coalter seeks to redress a historiographical bias in Great Awakening scholarship, which has focused excessively on New England and overlooked the importance of the Pietist tradition and Middle Colony Awakeners like Tennent. Coalter's analysis ascribes equal theological influence to Tennant's father, William, and to the Dutch Reformed clergyman Theodorus Frelinghuysen. Tennent incorporated a Pietist perspective on the process of salvation into his revivalist approach, preaching terrors, emphasizing sincere practical piety over theological orthodoxy, judging the spiritual condition of other ministers, and disregarding their theological pedigrees. His opponents suspected that he was willing to sacrifice Presbyterian theology and order to promote the New Birth.

Blauvelt's paper describes the efforts of Presbyterians, through the 1830s, to achieve the revival without disturbing church order and discipline as the First Great Awakening's itinerants had. That Awakening had familiarized the laity with religious emotion, provided an outlet for it, and left a desire for further revivals. Later revivals developed a safe framework for that zeal—the prayer meeting—and an institutional means of maintaining control. A board of elders oversaw the spiritual state of the congregation; the minister kept his flock on the right theological track by preaching to the prayer meeting on experiential religion. Gone were the itinerants and the disorder which accompanied them. Ministers undertook preaching tours—but only at the direction of the presbytery. By the 1830s the revival had achieved set stages wherein prayer meetings would burgeon into orderly, controlled revivals. The First Awakening exalted the evangelist; the Second spread authority between minister and laity. While ministers got along more harmoniously with their congregations in the Second Awakening, they never recovered the authority they had held before 1730. Moreover, the change in revival form raised the problem of Arminianism. The new structure lent credence to the idea that God was responsive to human needs. The role of the laity made grace seem all the more the result of human effort.

In his commentary Paul Johnson suggests that the scope of both papers is somewhat limited, because, he suggests, information is scarce on New Jersey society in this period. The kind of information which underlies the sophisticated studies of New England and the Chesapeake is simply not available for New Jersey. Therefore it is much more difficult to investigate beyond the boundaries of traditional church history. Both authors have contributed new knowledge about the period; both need to pose additional questions about the societies under examination.

The Quakers remained aloof from the Awakening. Friends had similar problems dealing with evangelicalism or enthusiasm—both with the Keithian schism of the 1690s and later with the Hicksite movement of the 1820s. However, as Jean Soderlund's study of two Delaware Valley Quaker meetings illustrates, slavery was the central question of importance to Quakers before the Revolution. Although Quakers did not initially present a united front on this question, they faced it nearly a century before other Protestant denominations, and avoided the disruptions which split the Methodists, Presbyterians and Baptists into northern and southern churches in the 1830s and 1840s.

Chesterfield and Shrewsbury meetings both finally barred slavery, but many years separated their decisions. Shrewsbury took an antislavery position in the 1750s and was in the forefront of the abolitionist group within the Philadelphia Yearly Meeting. Chesterfield reached an abolitionist position only after the issuance of the directive of 1776. While a variety of economic factors affected the ways the two meetings approached the slavery problem, Soderlund's analysis shows that there were also distinct differences in the ways they handled their members. Shrewsbury meeting placed more emphasis on persuading its members to manumit their slaves; its members generally freed their slaves in their wills. Chesterfield did nothing until the Yearly Meeting's directive and until after most of its slaveholders had left positions of leadership, left the meeting or died. Once Chesterfield reached an antislavery position, it moved quickly against remaining slaveholders. It disowned them, showing more interest in strict adherence to the meeting discipline itself than in the purpose of the directive—freedom for blacks. The meetings dealt with the other major problem of discipline, marrying outside the meeting, as they had the problem of slavery. Shrewsbury showed little interest in disciplining those who married out. Chesterfield disciplined its members—even before the Yearly Meeting decided to tighten discipline in 1755.

Douglas Jacobsen suggests a wider context in which to study the history of religion in New Jersey. The religious conflict and denominational diversity which are detailed in most studies of colonial New Jersey have obscured the general allegiance among New Jerseyans to a common set of beliefs. Colonists in New Jersey, like most people throughout the Protestant world, held certain ideas in common and expressed them in the rhetoric of Protestant Christianity. God's favor was conditional on the nation's purity; that purity could and should be enforced by law and institutions. Jacobsen defines this as a religiously grounded sense of community or an informal establishment of religion. He notes that the emphasis subsequently changed. Community, rather than being imposed by law, was recast in the language of unity. While all were not and could not be alike, all should be united for the common good. Jacobsen believes that this community of ideas helps explain why toleration flourished as the eighteenth century progressed.

John F. Wilson suggests that the kind of analysis Jean Soderlund employs might profitably be applied to other, similar Quaker communities. Perhaps more might be made of the different origins of these Quaker societies. Wilson finds that Jacobsen has suggested a stimulating line of research. While he has begun to make a case that a residual religious tone pervaded the community of New Jersey, full verification will require the examination of more data.

As these papers make clear, New Jersey was a microcosm. Its borders contained most of the major Protestant denominations and, in later years, large numbers of Catholics as well. Because most early American religious conflicts or movements affected New Jersey or took place within its borders, the state is an ideal subject for the study of religious history.

Many members of the Commission staff have made important contributions to this book. Diane E. Dillon, Judith Morello and Patricia A. Thomas produced an accurate text of the introduction and papers with their accustomed efficiency. Howard L. Green and Richard Waldron made helpful editorial suggestions. Lee R. Parks ably guided the volume through the editorial stage. Nancy H. Dallaire efficiently handled the details of design and production. We owe a special note of thanks to the chairman of the Commission, Henry Drewry, who presided over the symposium itself.

Notes

1. Because Catholics and Jews did not begin to arrive in great numbers until the 1850s, we will confine our discussion to the Protestant denominations.

The statistics on church numbers, areas of concentration and population figures are drawn from information in Nelson R. Burr, *The Anglican Church in New Jersey* (Philadelphia, 1954); Lester Cappon, ed., *Atlas of Early American History: The Revolutionary Era 1760–1790* (Princeton, 1976), pp. 36, 38; Edward T. Corwin, *A Manual of the Reformed Church in America,* 3rd ed. (New York, 1879), pp. 571–646; Edwin Scott Gaustad, *Historical Atlas of Religion in America,* rev. ed., (New York, 1976), p. 176; Thomas F. Gordon, *Gazetteer of the State of New Jersey* (1834, Cottonport, La.: 1973), pp. 73–84; Jedediah Morse, *The American Universal Geography* (Boston, 1802), pp. 513–4; U.S. Bureau of the Census, *Historical Statistics of the United States, Colonial Times to 1970* (Washington, 1975), v. 1, p. 31, v. 2, pp. 1168, 1170; Peter O. Wacker, *Land and People: A Cultural Geography of Preindustrial New Jersey* (New Brunswick, 1975), chap. 3; Frederick Weis, *The Colonial Churches and the Colonial Clergy of the Middle and Southern Colonies, 1607–1776* (Lancaster, Mass.: 1938). These figures are fairly general, and totals given by these authorities often vary; the numbers should be read as suggestive of trends rather than as exact. See table 1.

2. No exact figure for the number of Methodist churches in 1830 was obtainable. Methodists are figured at two churches per minister, in accordance with the information in Gordon, *Gazetteer.* If a lower number of churches is assumed, the rate of growth from 1830 to 1850 is even more dramatic.

Quaker Abolitionism in Colonial New Jersey: The Shrewsbury and Chesterfield Monthly Meetings

Jean R. Soderlund

Jean Ruth Soderland is the curator of the Peace Collection at Swarthmore College in Pennsylvania. She is the editor of *William Penn and the Founding of Pennsylvania, 1680–84: A Documentary History*, and has served on the editorial staff of the *Papers of William Penn*, volumes 1 and 2. She is investigating the manumission of slaves in eighteenth-century Pennsylvania.

EIGHTEENTH-CENTURY American Quakers are generally viewed as a homogeneous group. In most American colonies they were a small and often persecuted sect. They are famous as the first organized religion to forbid members to own slaves. Historians who have studied the development of abolitionism in the Philadelphia Yearly Meeting—the central body to which Friends from New Jersey, Pennsylvania, and parts of Delaware and Maryland belonged—have focused primarily on prominent Philadelphia Quakers. In debating the question of why Friends came to oppose slavery sooner than people of other religions, these scholars have used evidence about the behavior of the Philadelphia merchant elite exclusively without looking in depth at the words and actions of Friends in other places in the Delaware Valley.[1] Study of two local meetings in New Jersey, the Shrewsbury and Chesterfield monthly meetings, shows that different groups of Quakers reached the conclusion that slavery was wrong at widely variant times in the colonial period. It also sheds light on the process, and the influences on that process, by which individual Friends and their meetings approached their decisions.

Slavery was an extremely controversial issue for the Quakers of the Shrewsbury and Chesterfield meetings, as it was for their co-religionists throughout the Delaware Valley. On the one hand, many Friends employed slaves on their farms, in their shops and other places of business, and in their homes. For Quaker slave owners, blacks were a sizable part of their estates and provided what they considered to be essential labor. On the other hand, slavery troubled Friends on moral and religious grounds. Quakerism had three basic tenets that proponents of abolitionism could employ to support their case. The first was that all people, men and women of whatever ethnic or national origin, were equal in the sight of God. Friends who were not sympathetic to abolitionism argued that this meant that everyone was capable of receiving God's light, not that all humans should be equal socially, politically, and economically. Probably no Quaker abolitionist believed that blacks were the social equals of whites, and most reformers accepted without comment the hierarchical social and political structure of the eighteenth century. They believed slavery was wrong because under the system of involuntary bondage one person could force another to do his or her will; thus masters could prevent their slaves from reaching God. Slave

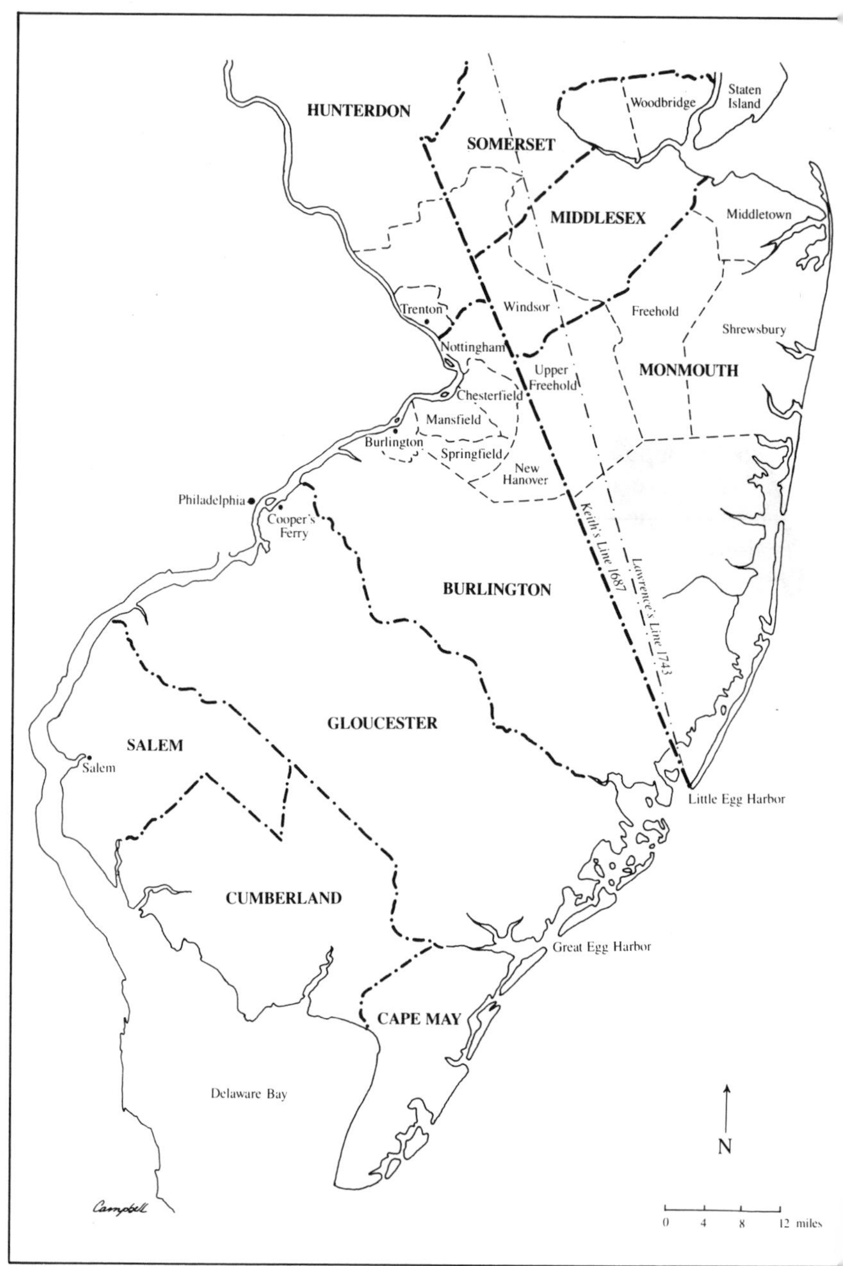

Central and Southern New Jersey, 1775. *Based on John P. Snyder,* The Story of New Jersey's Civil Boundaries, 1606-1968 *(Trenton: Bureau of Geology and Topography, 1969), pp. 20-21.*

owners, for example, often separated husbands from wives, and thereby practically forced them to commit adultery.

The second tenet that Quaker abolitionists used to back their case was nonviolence. Proslavery apologists argued that they treated their slaves well and of course never beat them, but activists like John Hepburn, Benjamin Lay, John Woolman, and Anthony Benezet pointed out that Africans were captured by force and that the system of slavery could not exist without the use or threat of violence. The third Quaker doctrine was that Friends should avoid ostentation and sloth in their daily lives. Abolitionists accused slaveholders of using their blacks as symbols of conspicuous consumption; they also thought that slavery made both masters and their children lazy.

Thus slavery was an issue that required Friends in the Delaware Valley to weigh carefully the implications of their religious beliefs in their daily lives. Since George Fox and other early English Friends had not specifically banned slavery, a new rule against the institution had to be hammered out within the American meetings if the reform was to be effected. From 1688, when the Germantown Quakers wrote the first antislavery petition, until the mid-eighteenth century, abolitionists succeeded only in convincing the Philadelphia Yearly Meeting to urge members to treat their slaves well and to avoid participating in the slave trade. The Yearly Meeting made more substantial moves only in 1754 when it denounced slaveholding, in 1758 when it established penalities for buying and selling slaves, and in 1776 when it forbade slaveholding altogether. Abolitionism progressed in the Yearly Meeting as increasing numbers of Delaware Valley Friends adopted the attitude that slavery was wrong. The turning point came in the 1750s, when a new group of leaders gained the fore. Unlike their predecessors, they were opposed to slavery.

Hiding behind this very general pattern of growing abolitionism in the Yearly Meeting, however, are the varied experiences of local meetings. Shrewsbury Friends opposed slavery considerably earlier than most other local meetings in New Jersey and Pennsylvania, and Chesterfield purposefully lagged behind. The Shrewsbury meeting was in the forefront of the attack on slavery, while the Chesterfield meeting helped to postpone the final ban on slaveholding in the Yearly Meeting for over twenty years. These conflicting positions arose from differences in the importance of slavery to influential members of each meeting and from variations in the way each group interpreted Quaker thought.

Analysis of similarities and differences in the history of the Shrewsbury and Chesterfield meetings enables us to evaluate several hypotheses concerning the source of antislavery thought. Neither Quaker group was a persecuted minority in its home locality; both had members who belonged to the socioeconomic and political elite. A considerable number in both meetings owned slaves. However, the Shrewsbury meeting was established almost twenty years before its counterpart in West Jersey, the Shrewsbury Friends formed a smaller proportion of the population in their locale, and slavery became entrenched at an earlier date and to a much greater extent in the eastern Monmouth County area around Shrewsbury than in the Chesterfield area. In addition, the founders of Shrewsbury meeting immigrated to New Jersey from Long Island and Rhode Island while most early Chesterfield Friends came directly from England. By examining the influence of these factors on the widely variant growth of abolitionism in Shrewsbury and Chesterfield, we can gain a better insight into the differing ways in which colonial New Jersey Quakers applied their religious principles in their daily lives.

IN 1665, A GROUP of Long Island Quakers and Baptists arrived in eastern Monmouth County, where they established two New England-style towns, Shrewsbury and Middletown. They had purchased a large triangle of land from the Lenni Lenape that extended from Sandy Hook to Barnegat Bay to a point on the Raritan River twenty-five miles west of its mouth; they obtained what was called the Navesink Patent for this area from Governor Richard Nicolls on April 4, 1665. Additional settlers arrived from Rhode Island, Long Island, and Massachusetts during the next few years, and by 1673 Shrewsbury and Middletown each had about 300 inhabitants. Most of the Baptist immigrants staked out their farms in Middletown, where they founded the first Baptist Church in New Jersey in 1688. Though some of the Friends stayed in Middletown, most went to Shrewsbury. They established their meeting soon after their arrival and built a meeting house in 1672.[2] George Fox, the founder of the Society of Friends, described his 1672 visit to the settlement in his journal. He and his companions arrived at Middletown harbor from Long Island and then traveled

> about 30: miles in the new Country through the woods very bad boggs, one worse then all, where wee and our horses was faine to slither downe a steepe place, & lett them to lie & breath themselves, & they call this purgatory; And soe wee came to Shrewsberry, & on the first day of the weeke we had a pretious Meetinge.[3]

The Quakers migrated to East Jersey at least in part to escape persecution in New England and New York. As founders of Shrewsbury, they participated in the provincial government from the very beginning. Fox marveled that in Shrewsbury "a friende is made A Justice." Eliakim Wardell, a Quaker minister who with his wife had appeared almost naked as a "sign" in the Hampton, New Hampshire, church, was elected one of three deputies from Shrewsbury to the Monmouth "assembly" in 1667. Several early Shrewsbury Friends were members of the Provincial Assembly, including Jedidiah Allen, who was elected in 1703 to the first assembly convened under the royal government, and Richard Hartshorne, who served from 1703 to 1707. And though the immigration to Monmouth County of Dutch settlers from Long Island and of Scottish ex-servants from Amboy circa 1700 quickly reduced the percentage of Quakers in the population, Friends remained part of the political elite of Monmouth County until the Revolution. John Eaton (served 1727–51), Richard Lawrence (1761–69 and 1772–76), and Robert Hartshorne (1769–72), all Shrewsbury Friends, represented the Monmouth County constituency in the New Jersey Assembly for much of the colonial period.[4]

Quakers were also well represented among the socioeconomic elite of eastern Monmouth County, as indicated by analysis of all surviving probate records for Middletown and Shrewsbury townships in the periods 1715–39 and 1764–80.[5] In the wealthiest 30 percent of the inventoried estates in the early period, almost one-half of the decedents whose religion could be identified were Friends. In the 1760s and 1770s, one-third of this elite group was Quaker.[6] Like their affluent neighbors of other religions, Friends employed slaves on their plantations. During the period 1715–39, over 85 percent of the Quaker decedents in the wealthiest 30 percent owned slaves—slightly higher than the percentage of all decedents in the same wealth category (see Table 1).

TABLE 1

SLAVE OWNERSHIP AND RELIGION AMONG WEALTHIEST 30 PERCENT OF INVENTORIED DECEDENTS IN SHREWSBURY MONTHLY MEETING AREA

	1715–39		1764–80	
	No.	Slave Owners (%)	No.	Slave Owners (%)
Quakers	7	85.7	6	16.7
Anglicans	2	100.0	3	100.0
Presbyterians	0		2	100.0
Baptists	4	75.0	3	100.0
Dutch Reformed	2	50.0	4	75.0
Religion unknown	6	83.3	5	40.0
Total	21	81.0	23	60.9

SOURCES: Probate, church, and meeting records (see notes 5, 6).

Some Shrewsbury Friends had probably brought black slaves with them when they came to New Jersey. In any event, many owned them by the time they died in the early eighteenth century. For example, Sarah Reape, widow of William Reape, who had once been deputy governor of Rhode Island and who with John Tilton of Gravesend, Long Island, had negotiated the Navesink purchase, owned eight slaves when she died in 1715.[7] One-half of the most active members of the Shrewsbury Monthly Meeting who died before 1741 owned slaves at death (see Table 2).[8] As part of the New York hinterland, the Shrewsbury area had greater access to blacks than most other local monthly meeting areas in New Jersey and Pennsylvania. Beginning particularly in the second decade of the eighteenth century, substantial numbers of slaves were imported into New York. Residents of the Shrewsbury area took advantage of this supply of labor, especially because relatively few white indentured servants were available. Data from the probate inventories for Shrewsbury and Middletown townships indicates a substantial increase in the percentage of decedents who owned blacks in the decade 1711–20; at that time the proportion owning slaves soared to almost 35 percent. The percentage owning slaves surpassed 36 percent in the 1720s and then declined to about 30 percent for the rest of the colonial period. In comparison with other parts of New Jersey and Pennsylvania, blacks were quite numerous in Monmouth County. For example, the New Jersey census of 1738 showed that blacks were 10.6 percent of the

TABLE 2

Slave Ownership Among Shrewsbury Monthly Meeting Participants

Date of Death	No.	Slave Owners (%)
1681–1700	0	
1701–20	6	50.0
1721–40	6	50.0
1741–60	22	27.3
1761–80	20	0.0
Total	54	22.2

Sources: Probate records; Shrewsbury MM minutes, 1732–80; Shrewsbury QM minutes, 1705–80; Philadelphia YM minutes, 1681–1780.

population of Monmouth County, compared with 6.5 percent of the population in Burlington County.[9]

The huge upsurge in slave imports in the 1710s and the widespread purchase of black labor by Friends and non-Friends alike prompted a quick reaction from at least one abolitionist. John Hepburn, a Scot living near Freehold in Monmouth County, considered himself a Quaker, but his standing among Friends is unclear. In 1714 Hepburn wrote one of the earliest abolitionist tracts published in America, *The American Defence of the Christian Golden Rule, or an Essay to Prove the Unlawfulness of Making Slaves of Men.* In this essay, he argued that slavery was inconsistent with Christianity and violated the golden rule. He indicted Presbyterian, Anabaptist, and Anglican preachers and laymen in his locality for owning slaves. As for the Quakers, Hepburn charged that while no Christian sect was stricter in other principles and practices, "no group of people [were] more forward in making slaves of men."[10]

Hepburn's tract, though possibly exaggerated on some points, presents an enlightening portrait of slavery in early eighteenth-century East Jersey. In addition it elucidates the ways in which the institution offended sensitive Friends. Slave owners, according to Hepburn, could enrich themselves without physical labor, and keep their hands clean except when blood-spattered from beating their slaves. These masters could afford to wear fine powdered wigs and greatcoats, and their wives had time to paint their faces and puff and powder their hair. Their children grew up in idleness. In contrast, according to Hepburn, their slaves were clothed with rags, or with no clothes or shoes even in the winter. Some slaves were forced either to lie in the ashes of the fire or to live in huts outside. Slaves were given names like those of dogs or horses—Toby, Jack, and Hector—and some were forced to punish or hang fellow blacks. Hepburn believed that the separation of husbands from wives and of children from parents was an especially bad aspect of slavery that forced adult blacks to commit adultery and made children unable to honor their parents. He attributed the suicide in 1712 of a black in his neighborhood to the poor treatment generally afforded slaves in East Jersey.[11]

While it is uncertain that John Hepburn convinced weighty members of the Shrewsbury Monthly Meeting that slavery was inconsistent with Quaker ideals, East Jersey Friends were becoming concerned about the growth of slavery in their locality by the 1720s. The minutes of the meeting are missing before 1732, and are silent on the subject of slavery and the slave trade until 1757; but there is evidence that the meeting developed an antislavery position independent of the Philadelphia Yearly Meeting before the 1750s. The meeting sent no official petitions to the Yearly Meeting, and no abolitionist pamphlets written by confirmed meeting members exist. Quaker records do, however, reveal that Shrewsbury Friends opposed the slave trade by 1730, for in that year the Shrewsbury Quarterly Meeting agreed with the petition put forward by the Chester Quarterly Meeting to prohibit members from buying imported blacks.[12] Because only one other meeting (Woodbridge) belonged to the Shrewsbury Quarter, the agreement of the Shrewsbury Friends was almost certainly necessary for the quarterly meeting to reach this decision.

Other evidence of an early antislavery movement among Shrewsbury Quakers comes from the wills of deceased Friends. Simeon Moss found in his analysis of the abstracts of New Jersey wills that Shrewsbury residents led the colony in emancipation by will. Indeed, a study of the probate records themselves reveals that in 1720, John Lippincott, a weighty Shrewsbury Friend and slave owner, began the process by making provision to free his "Negro man Oliver" in his will. He was followed with increasing frequency by other Quaker slave owners. In the 1715–39 sample of all Middletown and Shrewsbury probate records (see Table 3), thirty (26.5 percent) of the 113 decedents who left wills and/or inventories owned slaves. Ten, or one-third, of these slave owners can be identified as Quakers; in their wills four of these Friends freed all their slaves, while another freed one of the several he owned. More specifically, of the four slave-owning Quakers in this sample who died in the 1730s, only one failed to manumit his slaves. In contrast to the Friends, only one local non-Quaker slave owner made freedom possible for his slaves in his will. Elias Mestayer, a French Protestant who had no wife or children when he died in 1731, provided that the black husband and wife he owned should operate his plantation for five years and then be freed.[13] The Quaker emancipationist movement in Shrewsbury was even stronger among the Friends who took an active role in their monthly meeting. Seven of eight slave-owning leaders who died after 1725 but before 1761 freed their slaves in their wills.

Several questions arise concerning the depth and scope of antislavery sentiment among these Friends. Most of the wills, for example, either deferred the freedom of the blacks or required them to make yearly payments to the decedents' heirs. John Lippincott, the first emancipator, gave the use of his black man to his wife during her life and then to his two sons for one and one-half years each. The sons, John and Preserve, were then directed to sell Oliver in either New York or Pennsylvania for ten days, after which he was to be free for the rest of his life. Joseph Wardell, who died in 1735, also freed his slaves Jack and Joany only after his wife's death. Other Friends deferred emancipation until the blacks reached age thirty or thirty-five years. George Williams, Sr., deceased in 1744, freed his mulatto man James McCarty at age thirty.

TABLE 3

SLAVE OWNERSHIP AND RELIGION AMONG DECEDENTS IN SHREWSBURY MONTHLY MEETING AREA

	1715–30		1731–39		1764–80	
	No.	Slave Owners (%)	No.	Slave Owners (%)	No.	Slave Owners (%)
Quakers	23	26.1	15	26.7	32	6.2
Anglicans	2	0.0	7	28.6	26	26.9
Presbyterians	1	100.0	2	100.0	6	50.0
Baptists	4	50.0	5	40.0	13	30.8
Dutch Reformed	4	50.0	6	33.3	15	53.3
French Protestant	0		1	100.0	0	
Religion unknown	23	13.0	20	15.0	53	18.9
Total	57	24.6	56	28.6	145	23.4

SOURCES: Probate, church, and meeting records (see notes 5, 6).

McCarty would receive freedom dues of a horse under seven years old and two suits of clothes (one new); but if he were to "take bad ways" and incur charges against the estate, the executors were free to sell him. John Lippincott, Jr., freed his black woman Hesther immediately upon his death in 1747; but her five children, aged sixteen to twenty-nine, were each required to serve until age thirty-five. They were also warned to behave themselves if they expected to be freed. Two other Friends, Thomas White, Sr., (died 1747) and Dr. Walter Harbert (died 1755), freed their black men immediately, but required James and Sesar to pay an annual sum (£5 and £2 respectively), which would be used if they became unable to support themselves.[14]

One might reasonably ask whether Shrewsbury Friends were truly in the forefront of the Quaker antislavery movement if manumitting owners deferred freedom and required annual payments. A 1769 entry from the diary of the premier Quaker abolitionist, John Woolman, explains the Friends' reasons for such restrictions, and even suggests that Woolman found the reasons acceptable, at least until that year.

> As persons setting Negroes free in our province are bound by law to maintain them in case they have need of relief, some who scrupled keeping slaves term of life (in the time of my youth) were wont to detain their young Negroes in their service till thirty years of age, without wages, on that account. And with this custom I so far agreed that I, as companion to another Friend in executing the will of a deceased Friend, once sold a Negro lad till he might attain the age of thirty years and applied the money to the use of the estate.[15]

The 1714 New Jersey law to which Woolman referred required that a "Master or Mistress manumitting and setting at Liberty any Negro or Mulatto Slave, shall enter into sufficient Security unto her Majesty, her Heirs and Successors, with two Sureties, in the Sum of Two Hundred Pounds" in order to prevent the freed blacks from becoming "a Charge to the Place where they are." The executors of wills made by testators who desired to free their slaves were required to post bonds for the ex-slaves' support.[16] Thus, in demanding deferred freedom or annual payments from their slaves, the manumitting Friends were attempting to ensure that the support of freed blacks would not become a burden on their estates. That New Jersey Friends emancipated their slaves in spite of this extremely high surety bond is compelling evidence of the strength of their opposition to slavery.

The intensity of antislavery fervor among Shrewsbury Friends might be further questioned because these slave-owning Quakers freed their slaves only after their deaths, thus reaping the benefits of slavery themselves and depriving only their heirs. We don't know how many Quakers may have freed their slaves during their lives, but analysis of probate inventories indicates that slaveholding itself declined markedly among Quakers after 1740. Friends in the Shrewsbury area stopped buying slaves and freed those they owned before their deaths. Of the six Quakers whose estates ranked in the wealthiest 30 percent of all inventories for Shrewsbury and Middletown between 1764 and 1780 only one, William Woolley, owned slaves, and he freed them in his will, probated in 1769 (see Table 1). Catherine Hartshorne, whose estate did not rank in the top 30 percent, owned a black girl, Dinah, whom she freed when she died in 1767. From 1741 to 1760, fewer than one-third of the probated Quaker participants in the monthly meeting owned slaves at their deaths, and none who died during the years 1761–80 owned slaves at death (see Table 2). By the 1760s, the difference between wealthy Shrewsbury Friends and their upper-class neighbors is striking: eleven of the twelve non-Quaker decedents in the top 30 percent of inventoried estates owned slaves. Only one of these, an Anglican, freed her black man, William, in her will.[17]

The monthly meeting minutes reveal that some Shrewsbury Friends continued to own slaves into the 1770s. By the 1750s, however, the meeting had adopted an antislavery position. And when the Philadelphia Yearly Meeting decided that slave importing and buying, and then slaveholding itself, should be banned among its members, the Shrewsbury Monthly Meeting proceeded quickly, but judiciously, against its nonconforming members. Shrewsbury Friends pressed in the Yearly Meeting for increasing strictness in the discipline concerning slavery, and many of their discipline cases involved Friends who held blacks only for a term.

In 1757, when John Wardell bought a slave, the Shrewsbury Monthly Meeting requested the quarterly meeting's opinion concerning the "extensiveness" of the Yearly Meeting's minute prohibiting the importation or buying of blacks. The quarterly meeting, with the monthly meeting's approval, decided that if a Friend bought a slave and refused to make satisfaction by condemning the crime, then the monthly meeting had the authority to disown him. Shrewsbury was in fact the only quarterly meeting to decide on its own that slave buyers should be disowned. Indeed the next year the Yearly Meeting decided only to bar slave buyers from participating in monthly meetings or contributing funds.[18]

During the 1760s, several Shrewsbury Friends bought and sold slaves. In each case, the meeting required the offending member to provide for or obtain the freedom of the black. Although some of the slaves had to serve for a number of years—Thomas Wooley stated to the satisfaction of the meeting that he and the black man he bought had agreed before the purchase that the slave would be free after sixteen years—the meeting even expected members who sold slaves to obtain their freedom. Stephen Cook sold two blacks for term of life in 1764. When he was unable to buy them back and free them, he was testified against by the meeting. Before the 1770s, few other monthly meetings expected more than that their offending members apologize and promise not to deal in slaves again.[19]

In 1770, the Shrewsbury meeting extended the Yearly Meeting's position even further when it learned that several Friends, Brittain Corlies, Samuel Parker, William Parker, and William Jackson, had purchased blacks who would remain slaves past the age of twenty-one. A committee was appointed in 1772 to decide whether they had disobeyed the Yearly Meeting minute of 1758. This committee decided they had, the quarterly meeting agreed, and the erring members were required to obtain freedom for the blacks after their terms expired and to acknowledge their wrongdoing. In January 1774, the meeting continued its role in the antislavery vanguard by prohibiting Amos White of Deal from even hiring the labor of a slave.[20]

When the Philadelphia Yearly Meeting in 1774 instructed monthly meetings to appoint committees to treat with slave owners, Shrewsbury Friends selected a group of weighty Friends, who with the help of the quarterly meeting committee, visited slave-owning members. In their 1775 report, they found that nine members owned a total of twenty-four blacks. Of these slaves, thirteen were above the age that the Yearly Meeting specified for freedom (eighteen years for females, twenty-one years for males). Four of the slave owners, who held a total of twelve slaves (six above age), showed no disposition to give them education or freedom at any age. Four other Friends promised to free their adult slaves either immediately or after several years and to educate and free their slave children when of age. The ninth owner had hired a man from a non-Quaker, and had already made arrangements for the man to earn money to buy his freedom. The report also indicated that at least five of the slaves, including two adults and three children, had been taught to read.[21]

The committee reported again in 1776. By that time only Josiah Parker and Zilpha and John Corlies (the widow and son of the one monthly meeting leader who died after 1725 without freeing his slaves) refused to manumit or educate their slaves. John Stevenson was willing to free his two adult women, but could not "see his way clear to do it" because one was old and very infirm and the other had four young children. Robert, John, and Esek Hartshorne had freed or promised to free all their adult slaves by January 1, 1777, and the young ones were to be educated and freed at suitable ages. Richard Lawrence's black man had served his time and was now free. The appointed meeting members continued to treat with slave owners. By April 1778, only John Corlies refused to manumit his slaves, although John Stevenson, now deceased, had left his black women and children in such a situation that they could not legally be freed. In December 1778, Corlies was disowned, and by 1780 the meeting had procured (though with considerable effort) written manumissions for all slaves, over and under age, owned by meeting members.[22]

The drive of the Shrewsbury Monthly Meeting to enforce the discipline of the Yearly Meeting from the 1750s through the 1770s was a sincere effort to remove the last vestiges of slaveholding from the meeting. The issue was clearly not used in an opportunistic manner by an "out-group" as a means of gaining control of the meeting from a slaveholding elite. Although the only member disowned for holding slaves was the richest man on the Shrewsbury Township tax list in 1779, and although Table 4 shows that those who violated the discipline had considerably more land and assessed wealth than those who dealt with the violators, one faction in the meeting was not wielding the slave issue to oust a wealthier group from power.[23] The antislavery activists included the most important meeting leaders of the 1750s, 1760s, and 1770s: twenty-four of the thirty-one men (77.4 percent) who treated with people who disobeyed the antislavery discipline were officers of the meeting during those years.[24]

The absence of factional in-fighting in the meeting is further illustrated by the fact that the antislavery group even included three slave owners,

Robert and John Hartshorne and Richard Lawrence, who dealt with cases concerning slavery either before or after their particular offenses were brought before the meeting. John Hartshorne and Lawrence both treated with a slave buyer in 1769, and John Hartshorne was a member of the committee that in 1773 treated with the four men who had hired the labor of slaves. Before slave ownership itself was prohibited by the Yearly Meeting, the Shrewsbury meeting evidently had no aversion to appointing slave owners to visit slave traders or those who hired the labor of slaves.

After the ruling against owning blacks was made in 1774, Shrewsbury Friends made some changes in the committee appointments. Lawrence was no longer given committee assignments, even though he had played a very active role in the meeting since 1763, and John Hartshorne participated on only one committee (to keep order at the quarterly meeting) between 1774 and November 1776, by which time he had freed or agreed to free his slaves. Both men returned to active duty in 1777, and Robert Hartshorne became a leader of the meeting in the late 1770s, after he had freed his slaves. Robert Hartshorne dealt with John Corlies,

TABLE 4

WEALTH AND LANDHOLDINGS OF MONTHLY MEETING PARTICIPANTS

	Number on Tax Lists	Landowners (%)	Landholdings (Av. Acreage)	Average Assessment (NJ Pounds)[a]
Shrewsbury (1779)				
All participants	59	83.0	154.8	42.3
Antislavery participants	21	95.2	177.6	53.3
Slave owners & traders	18	100.0	249.2	83.8
Chesterfield (1774, 1778-79)[b]				
All participants				
1778–79 only	102	—	—	91.8
1774, 78–79	107	81.3	229.0	—
Antislavery participants				
1778–79 only	25	—	—	96.2
1774, 78–79	27	85.2	187.5	—
Slave owners & traders				
1778-79 only	35	88.6	222.5	112.8

SOURCES: Shrewsbury MM minutes, 1732–80; Chesterfield MM minutes, 1684–1780; tax assessment lists.

[a]Adjusted; see note 23.

[b]Some Chesterfield participants were on the 1774 tax lists but not on the 1778–79 tax lists. Their landholdings are included here but their assessments are not.

the meeting's one recalcitrant slave owner, in 1778. Thus, while the Shrewsbury meeting followed the Yearly Meeting's advice of 1774 by not employing slave owners "in the Service of Truth," it did not use the slavery issue as a means of removing slaveholders from power permanently.[25]

The movement to eradicate slave trading and slave ownership in the Shrewsbury Monthly Meeting after 1756 therefore involved no upheavals nor even a change of policy. The large majority of the meeting elite simply used, and even stretched a bit, the new power given them by the Yearly Meeting to pull the last holdouts belonging to their meeting into the antislavery fold. The aim of the meeting was to end slaveholding among its members in any form. Its leaders did not use the issue as a front for a power struggle during the period from the 1750s to the 1770s. There is no evidence, because of the loss of records before 1732 and the silence of the minutes after that date on the issue of slavery, whether such a struggle had occurred earlier.

Shrewsbury Friends, then, developed a straightforward stand against slavery before the Philadelphia Yearly Meeting as a whole. Almost all meeting leaders who died owning slaves after 1725 freed them in their wills, and most Quakers who did not participate in meeting business followed their example. Slave ownership among Shrewsbury Friends declined to the extent that after 1760 no deceased leaders owned slaves at death, and only two Quakers (nonparticipants) owned slaves at death. The meeting opposed slave trading in 1730, supported disownment for slave traders in 1757 (before the Yearly Meeting), and required those who sold slaves to buy them back and free them. Shrewsbury Friends conscientiously disciplined errant members according to the meeting's interpretation of the Yearly Meeting rules, but did so in a fashion that suggests that little strife and no change of policy took place after 1756. These East Jersey Quakers initiated their antislavery program well before 1750 by freeing their own slaves rather than by telling others to free theirs, and even after 1756 Shrewsbury Friends were more interested in obtaining eventual freedom for blacks than in punishing offending Friends. All members who bought, sold, or hired the labor of slaves were required to provide for their freedom (even when non-Quakers actually owned the slaves), and the meeting patiently tried to obtain manumissions for every black man, woman, and child on whom meeting members had any claim. Only one obstinate member was disowned for holding slaves.

In contrast, the members of Chesterfield Monthly Meeting in West Jersey steadfastly resisted abolitionist reform. Although John Woolman made several official visits to families of that meeting and maintained friendship and acquaintance with many of its members, the Chesterfield meeting refused to discipline slave traders until after 1770.[26] One possible explanation for their refusal lay in the fact that many Chesterfield leaders of the 1750s and 1760s owned slaves. However, since weighty Shrewsbury Friends had also held slaves while at the same time opposing the purchase of imported blacks in 1730 and manumitting their own slaves, a more satisfying explanation must be sought.

The Chesterfield Monthly Meeting was founded primarily by Friends who migrated to Burlington County from England in the late 1670s and early 1680s. The population of the area remained predominantly Quaker well into the eighteenth century, and Friends were influential in the provincial government throughout the colonial period, even though they were politically dominant in West Jersey for only a short time under the proprietors. In 1705 Lord Cornbury "complained of the political machinations of the Quaker members of the Assembly who held all but two of the seats for West Jersey," and Lewis Morris attributed the difficulty of forming a militia in West Jersey to the cohesive resistance of the Friends. Active members of the Chesterfield Monthly Meeting who were representatives to the Assembly included Thomas Lambert (1703–07, 1709–16, 1721–30), William Biddle (1703–04), Joshua Wright (1704–07, 1730–38), Jacob Doughty (1716–21), William Cooke (1738–54), Daniel Doughty (1743–46, 1761–69), Samuel Wright (1745–49), Barzillai Newbold (1751–57), Joseph Bullock (1769–72), and Anthony Sykes (1772–76). Francis Davenport was a member of the Provincial Council from August 1702 until his death in 1708. Many Friends were active as township and county officials as well.[27] Thus, Friends in Chesterfield, like those in Shrewsbury, took an active role in provincial politics. The contrasting attitudes toward slavery of these meetings therefore cannot be linked to any differences in their ability to influence governmental policy.

As late as 1739, Quakers also dominated the socioeconomic elite in the townships of the Chesterfield meeting that have been selected for this study (see note 5, paragraph 2). Between 1730 and 1739, all of the wealthiest 30 percent of decedents whose estates were inventoried, and who can be identified by religion, were Quakers. This preponderance was reduced in the 1760s and 1770s as members of other religions moved into the Chesterfield Monthly Meeting area and as former Friends joined other churches. Still, Quakers made up 70 percent of inventoried decedents whose religion could be identified, and at least 47 percent of all the inventoried decedents in the selected Burlington County townships. The proportion of Quakers in the highest 30 percent decreased much more in Upper Freehold than in Burlington County, primarily because many wealthy Baptists, Dutch Reformed, and Presbyterians moved to Upper Freehold from eastern Monmouth County around 1700.[28]

Slavery was considerably less extensive in the Chesterfield area than in Shrewsbury for most of the colonial period. Except during the 1740s, fewer than 20 percent of all inventoried decedents in the Chesterfield area townships owned slaves, while over 29 percent of Middletown and Shrewsbury decedents whose estates were inventoried between 1711 and 1780 owned blacks. Part of the explanation for this difference probably lies in the fact that many of the Friends who formed a great proportion of the inhabitants of Burlington County eschewed slaveholding; but a more abundant supply of indentured servants in West Jersey than in eastern Monmouth County also played a role.[29]

Even though slavery was less important in West Jersey society as a whole, the leaders and members of the Chesterfield Monthly Meeting did own slaves. Unlike most of their co-religionists in Shrewsbury, they held onto them into the 1770s. Few Chesterfield Quakers freed their slaves in their wills. Whereas in Shrewsbury three-fourths in the 1730s—and all in the 1760s and 1770s—of decedent Quaker slave owners freed their slaves in their wills (Table 3), no Chesterfield Quaker decedents freed their blacks from 1730 to 1739 and only two of six Quaker owners did so in the later period. In addition, Table 5 shows that as late as the 1760s and 1770s almost one-fourth of the deceased Quakers in Chesterfield whose estates were inventoried and ranked in the top 30

TABLE 5

SLAVE OWNERSHIP AND RELIGION AMONG WEALTHIEST 30 PERCENT OF INVENTORIED DECEDENTS IN CHESTERFIELD MONTHLY MEETING AREA

	1730–39		1766(64)–80[a]	
	No.	Slave Owners (%)	No.	Slave Owners (%)
Quakers	16	37.5	25	24.0
Disowned Quakers	0		2	50.0
Anglicans	0		5	20.0
Presbyterians	0		4	50.0
Baptists	0		3	100.0
Dutch Reformed	0		2	100.0
Religion unknown	4	0.0	16	31.2
Total	20	30.0	57	35.1

SOURCES: Probate, church, and meeting records (see notes 5, 6).
[a]Includes all inventories from the Burlington County townships for 1766–80 and from Upper Freehold Township, Monmouth County, for 1764–80.

percent of local wealth owned slaves. Table 6 indicates that over one-third (twelve of thirty-four) of the deceased slave owners in the area whose estates were probated during the 1760s and 1770s and whose religion could be identified still were Friends. Table 5 also suggests that slaveholding was not as pervasive among members of other religions in the Chesterfield area as it was among non-Friends in the Shrewsbury Monthly Meeting locality. Only one of five Anglicans whose estates were inventoried and ranked in the top 30 percent from 1766 to 1780 and one-half of the Presbyterians in the same wealth category in the Burlington townships and Upper Freehold owned slaves, although all of the Baptists and Dutch Reformed in the top 30 percent were slave owners. Thus, there is some evidence that reasons other than the opposition of Friends to slavery, including most prominently the availability of indentured servants, contributed to the relatively low incidence of slaveholding in West Jersey.

In addition, the pattern of slaveholding among deceased participants of the Chesterfield Monthly Meeting was much different from that found in Shrewsbury (see Tables 2, 7). The percentage of participants who owned slaves at death was similar in the two meetings through 1760, although fewer Chesterfield Friends who died between 1721 and 1740 owned slaves. The chief difference was that 15.2 percent of the Ches-

TABLE 6

SLAVE OWNERSHIP AND RELIGION AMONG DECEDENTS IN CHESTERFIELD MONTHLY MEETING AREA

	1730–39		1766(64)–80[a]	
	No.	Slave Owners (%)	No.	Slave Owners (%)
Quakers	40	22.5	84	14.3
Disowned Quakers	0		9	22.2
Anglicans	2	50.0	19	26.3
Presbyterians	0		14	35.7
Baptists	0		12	58.3
Dutch Reformed	0		4	75.0
Religion unknown	40	5.0	82	8.5
Total	82	14.6	224	18.3

SOURCES: Probate, church, and meeting records (see notes 5, 6).
[a]Includes all inventories from the Burlington County townships for 1766–80 and from Upper Freehold Township, Monmouth County, for 1764–80.

terfield participants who died after 1760 owned slaves, while none of the Shrewsbury leaders dying during those years was a slave owner. Furthermore, no slave-owning Chesterfield leader manumitted his slaves before 1746, and even after that year only five (27.8 percent) of the eighteen decedent slave-owning participants freed their slaves—in their wills or before death—compared with 75 percent after 1745 in Shrewsbury. Two of these five freed their blacks only after 1776, and the slaves of one were freed by the agreement of the majority of his heirs rather than by the testator himself.[30]

The reluctance of Chesterfield Friends to oppose slavery is also apparent in the monthly meeting minutes. They steadfastly rejected abolitionist reform until the 1770s. In May 1730, the meeting "calmly" considered the petition of Chester Friends to ban the purchase of imported blacks and appointed a committee of weighty Friends, including clerk of meeting Thomas Lambert, Benjamin Clark, Abraham Farrington, and Isaac Horner, to draw up the sense of the meeting. These Friends, two of whom were slave owners, reported to the quarterly meeting

> that as Friends both here and elsewhere have been in the Practice of it [purchasing imported blacks] for time past and many Friends differing in their Opinions from others in that matter: we think restricting Friends at this time and bringing Such as fall into the same thing under dealing as Offenders will not be convenient lest it create contention and uneasiness among them which Should be carefully avoided.[31]

The monthly meeting continued to oppose antislavery reform through

TABLE 7

Slave Ownership Among Chesterfield Monthly Meeting Participants

Date of Death	No.	Slave Owners (%)
1681–1700	9	22.2
1701–20	8	50.0
1721–40	20	25.0
1741–60	46	30.4
1761–80	46	15.2
Total	129	24.8

Sources: Probate records, Chesterfield MM minutes, 1684–1780.

1770, for although the meeting reported in many of its answers to the queries that members had in fact bought or sold slaves, no slave traders were disciplined by the meeting before 1771. In response to the question of whether any Friends had imported or bought slaves, Chesterfield Friends wrote in 1758 "mostly clear" (5th month) and "We dont know but what we are clear in them respects except one" (11th Month). In February 1759, the clerk wrote "Clear as far as we know except one but care is on the minds of friends to treat with him as soon as opportunity will admit." There is no indication that Friends ever found the opportunity in this case or in any other that came up during the 1750s and 1760s, although the meeting repeatedly reported it was "not all clear of purchasing negroes" through the 1760s. In 1771, one Friend was disciplined for a long list of offenses including marrying out, fornication, fighting, and buying blacks, but he acknowledged his guilt and remained a member. In 1772, the meeting again reported the sale of a slave but did not discipline the offender. The policy of the meeting was now starting to change, however. A committee to visit slaveholders was appointed in 1775 at the urging of the Philadelphia Yearly Meeting and the Burlington Quarterly Meeting, but its members found the service difficult. The report of 1775, signed by Stacy Potts, stated that they found "several friends disposed to set their Negroes free but most of those are discouraged from the apprehension of incumbrance which it might occasion to their outward estates and some few refuse at present."[32] Chesterfield slave owners were evidently using the manumission law requiring the security bond as an excuse—justifiable or not—to hold onto their slaves. One Trenton Friend, Mary Dury, had already emancipated two black men in 1774, but the committee to treat with slave owners made little progress until 1777 in securing additional manumissions. However, the meeting did discipline Thomas Woodward and his wife Susannah of Upper Freehold in 1776 for neglecting to attend religious meetings, buying a slave, and behaving in an unbecoming manner. Woodward frequented taverns and his wife's dress and conversation were unacceptable. So they were disowned until "they come to a sense of their misconduct manifesting the same in life and conversation and condemn it as our discipline directs."[33]

The committee at last secured manumissions from fifteen Chesterfield Friends in 1777 for thirty-two slaves, and obtained freedom for seven more blacks from five owners the following year. The committee in 1778 also reported the names of seven members who refused to free their slaves. Six of these Friends, and one other who sold a black man, were disowned. Josiah Appleton, the seventh owner, died before he was disowned; but his son John, who evidently inherited the slave, was disowned when he too rejected manumission. Ten more slaves were freed in 1779 by ten owners (one woman was jointly held by seven Friends from Stony Brook who probably acquired her by inheritance), and four more recalcitrant members were disowned in 1779–80.[34] But still the duties of the committee on slavery were not ended, for in the years 1779–82, the committee reported that a few blacks had not yet been freed. Manumissions for seven blacks were signed by six Friends in the years 1781 through 1783, however. At last the slavery committee could report in the latter year that no blacks were held in bondage except for two cases that were not under the meeting's control. These blacks were probably among the eleven manumitted from 1786 to 1797 after the deaths of slave-owning husbands and fathers who had been disowned by the meeting for slaveholding or other offenses and had refused to give up their slaves.[35]

In Chesterfield, then, the eradication of slavery in the monthly meeting was more difficult than in Shrewsbury. A major policy shift was necessary during the 1770s in order to comply with the Yearly Meeting discipline. This change was accomplished only after substantial resistance among leaders and members had been overcome. It is uncertain whether some leaders specifically used the slavery issue to gain control of the meeting from its slaveholding elite. But it is clear that the policy change was accompanied by some turnover in leadership whether caused by exclusion from power, change of residence, or death of the slave-owning leaders.

Between 1760 and 1777 eight participants in the monthly meeting, including officers Isaac Horner and Eliakim Hedger, died owning slaves; none of these men freed his blacks. Daniel Doughty, who almost continuously represented the monthly meeting at the quarterly meeting from 1748 until he moved to Burlington Monthly Meeting in 1776, died in 1778 owning a slave, but freed him in his will. Another weighty Friend, William Morris, who served on monthly meeting committees and as representative to the quarterly meeting from 1730 to 1773, freed a black woman and her child as late as 1774.[36] The loss of these men as leaders and the dropping out or exclusion by 1776 of seven of nine other slave owners who had participated in the monthly meeting before 1770 changed the balance of opinion in the meeting and permitted Friends who were more inclined to accept antislavery to take control. Each of the two slave owners who remained active in the meeting after 1776 manumitted his slave in 1777. Of the four slave owners who had not participated in the monthly meeting before 1770, only Thomas Thorne was assigned duties between 1775 and the manumission of his two young blacks in 1779. Two others did not become active until after they freed their slaves. As might be expected from this turnover, almost no slave owners participated on antislavery committees. The lone exception was

Robert White, who, with six other people from Stony Brook, manumitted a black woman, Susannah, in 1779. White became a participant in the monthly meeting and was assigned to treat with slaveholders only after the manumission was secured.[37]

The committees assigned by Chesterfield Monthly Meeting to treat with slaveholders during the late 1770s and early 1780s were different from those of Shrewsbury. Only 51.8 percent (fourteen of twenty-seven) were officers of the meeting in Chesterfield, whereas 77.4 percent (twenty-four of thirty-one) were officers in Shrewsbury. The reason for this difference was at least partly that the Shrewsbury committees were appointed over a longer period so that more officers could be involved. In Chesterfield, almost one-half (thirteen of twenty-seven) of the committee members were recruited from among men who had started performing tasks for the monthly meeting only after 1770. Stacy Potts (who became clerk of meeting in 1776), John Bullock, Anthony Sykes, Benjamin Field, Samuel Satterthwaite, Jr., and Abraham Skirm were older officers who started serving the monthly meeting in the era between the late 1740s and the early 1760s. They were joined by less experienced men who started out between 1767 and the early 1780s, including Fretwell Wright, Jacob Middleton, Barzillai Forman, Isaac Wright, Benjamin Linton, and Benjamin Clarke. Thus, the policy of the monthly meeting on slavery was reversed by a coalition of men who had served under the old regime and new men replacing slaveholders (and nonslaveholders) who had died or otherwise left their leadership positions by the early 1770s.[38] Given this continuity, it seems unlikely that the issue of slavery was used by the antislavery group as a way to gain power in the meeting, even though most slave owners were in some way removed from influence. As in Shrewsbury, some slave owners either assumed places of leadership or returned to them after they manumitted their slaves, and many of the antislavery proponents already had influential positions before 1776.

As in Shrewsbury, then, antislavery was debated on its own merits as a question about how Quakers should relate their religious ideals to their daily lives. Several Chesterfield leaders active throughout the eighteenth century had strong antislavery views. John Sykes was a well-respected Friend whose career in the meeting began in 1709. Sykes, who was appointed by the Philadelphia Yearly Meeting in 1758 to accompany John Woolman and three others on visits to slave owners, was quite possibly a constant source of irritation for slave owners. As executor of the will of Mathew Champion of the town of Burlington in 1735, he secured freedom for Jo, a black man who had belonged to the deceased. Sykes's own will set aside money to take care of the man in case he should become chargeable to Sykes's estate. Anthony Sykes, John's son and an antislavery leader of the monthly meeting, was appointed by his father to support the freed man if necessary. In 1760 the younger Sykes may have been instrumental in obtaining the agreement of William Cooke's heirs for the manumission of that deceased man's slave. In 1770 he served with other prominent antislavery Friends on the Yearly Meeting committee appointed to obtain freedom for the heirs of James McCarty, an ex-slave from Shrewsbury.[39]

In sum, the Chesterfield Monthly Meeting, like Shrewsbury, did genuinely oppose slavery when it finally started disciplining slave traders and owners. Unlike the Quakers of eastern Monmouth County, however, who had voiced their opposition to the importation of blacks as early as 1730 and were systematically manumitting their slaves in their wills before 1750, the Chesterfield meeting was able to reach a consensus against the institution only in the mid-1770s. What accounts for the wide difference in timing between these two meetings? Why was one moving earlier, the other later, than the Yearly Meeting as a whole? In each meeting, the success of the drive against slavery depended on two factors: the socioeconomic circumstances in which Friends made choices concerning slavery, and the members' beliefs about how Quaker teachings related to these practical concerns.

ANTISLAVERY reformers in the Society of Friends never contended that slavery was economically unsound in their efforts to convince slave masters to release their blacks. Their arguments emphasized instead the incompatibility of Christianity with owning slaves. Nevertheless, socioeconomic considerations did influence the debate over slavery within the meetings. Slave owners (and potential slave owners) could not avoid weighing the benefits of the Afro-Americans' labor, the value of their invested or inherited capital in slaves, and the cost of manumission bonds against the force of the reformers' ideals. The strength and effectiveness of the proslavery faction in each local meeting depended on the number and influence of slave owners and the steadfastness with which they held onto their slaves.

The differences in slave ownership patterns between Shrewsbury and Chesterfield have already been discussed. The eastern Monmouth County Quakers were heavily involved in slavery by the 1720s, but from that decade on, many leaders and members manumitted their slaves in their wills, and others avoided buying any blacks at all. By 1757, the Shrewsbury meeting had developed a clear-cut antislavery policy, and it used the Yearly Meeting decisions of 1758 and 1774 to force the few holdout slave owners to comply. Chesterfield Friends, on the other hand, do not appear to have enmeshed themselves in slavery as completely as the early Shrewsbury leaders. Subsequently, however, they held onto their slaves much later and even refused to accept the Yearly Meeting proscription on slave trading until the mid-1770s. A relatively large band of influential slaveholding Quakers kept the Chesterfield meeting out of the abolitionist camp.

The timing of the development of slavery in East and West Jersey helps explain why the behavior of these two meetings was so different. As discussed above, residents of East Jersey invested most heavily in slave labor before 1730. In the Chesterfield Monthly Meeting area, some early settlers owned slaves, but an increase in the residents' dependence on slavery turned up in the probate records only after the 1740s. Friends and their neighbors bought slaves as indentured servants grew scarce—especially during the Seven Years' War. By the 1750s the development of large farms and the increase in average wealth in both Burlington County and Upper Freehold Township in Monmouth County created a rising demand for slave labor.

Table 4 suggests that socioeconomic concerns affected the position on antislavery of participants in both local meetings. For instance, in Shrewsbury the average amount of land held by monthly meeting participants listed on the Shrewsbury and Middletown tax lists was significantly less than the acreage held by that proportion who owned or traded in slaves.[40] The slaveholders also held on average much more land than the antislavery group (who included most of the meeting leadership). The average acreage for the eighteen Quaker slave owners and traders was 249.2 acres—close to the average of all eastern Monmouth County slave owners of 283.7 acres as listed on the 1779 Shrewsbury and Middletown township tax assessments. Thus the Shrewsbury Friends who bought and held onto their slaves into the 1760s were large landowners who, like other slave owners of the locality, needed extra labor to work their farms. Although the average amount of land owned by Shrewsbury Quakers who had manumitted their slaves earlier is not known, it seems significant that such a wide gap existed between the average landholdings of the antislavery and slaveowning groups of the late 1750s through the 1780s. That many leading as well as ordinary Friends simply did not need additional labor probably facilitated their decision to oppose slavery.

In Chesterfield Monthly Meeting, on the other hand, the size of their landholdings did not make the acceptance of antislavery reform easier for the 107 participants who were listed on the 1774 and 1779 tax lists (Table 4). Comparison of the landholdings of all meeting participants who held land with those of slaveholding members who had farms shows that the meeting participants on average actually possessed slightly more land than the slave owners. Thus, many of the meeting participants of the 1740s through the 1770s who were still household heads in 1774 and 1779 were large farm owners, and their awareness of possible labor needs must have entered into their decision on whether to oppose slavery among their fellow Friends.

In short, in both Shrewsbury and Chesterfield, slave-owning Quakers—like most slaveholders in the two areas—owned large farms. The determination of many to hold onto their slaves surely stemmed from their need for additional labor. The significant difference between the two meetings in the average size of landholdings of all meeting participants thus accounts in part for their disagreement on antislavery. Most Shrewsbury Quakers held lands too small to require or support slave labor, but the majority of Chesterfield participants continued to own farms large enough to require extra labor as late as 1779.

In these ways, then, economic considerations affected the Quaker debate over slavery. Quaker farmers who continued to find slave labor useful resisted abolitionist reform. As long as these slave owners held influence in the meeting, as they did in Chesterfield until the mid-1770s, agreement in favor of antislavery could not be reached. The rapid growth of slavery in Shrewsbury in the early eighteenth century made the inconsistency of the institution with Quaker ideals very clear to Friends living there. Many came to believe that Robert Barclay's instructions to avoid violence, familiar to all Friends, extended to the force required to enslave blacks and keep them subordinated. Rumors of real and imagined slave rebellions in New York, South Carolina, and the West Indies certainly concerned pacifist Friends. And the daily struggle to force unpaid laborers and their children to work and behave, without using violence, must have taxed the imaginations of conscientious Quakers.[41] Thus, in Shrewsbury, the startling growth of slavery by the 1720s stirred the consciences of Friends to oppose the institution. In Chesterfield, to the contrary, since the black population remained small before 1750, few Friends were moved to oppose further development of slavery—especially because rapid development in the third quarter of the eighteenth century brought about a new need for labor just as alternative sources of free and bound immigrant labor shrank.

The concern of reform-minded Friends in Shrewsbury about the upsurge in slaveholding early in the eighteenth century and the contrasts between the later experiences of leading Friends in Shrewsbury and Chesterfield explain adequately the wide interval in the timing of the two meetings' acceptance of antislavery. But there was a difference in the ways these two groups enforced other items of the discipline that provokes further investigation. Their divergent views about how Friends should relate with outsiders suggest that the leaders of the meetings interpreted Quaker theology in two different ways—one that stressed humanitarianism and another that emphasized group cohesiveness. Both tendencies were securely rooted in the traditions of the Society of Friends.

In this vein, J. William Frost has suggested that there were two kinds of reformers in the Philadelphia Yearly Meeting in the 1750s: those who supported more stringent enforcement of the rules of marriage, and others who advocated antislavery and similar philanthropic concerns. In 1755 the Philadelphia Yearly Meeting decided to tighten the discipline against marrying members of other religions. This decision has been seen as evidence that Friends became more tribalistic in the wake of their loss of power in the Pennsylvania government. Frost hypothesizes that the Meeting's directive was advanced by Friends like John Churchman and Israel, James, and John Pemberton, who had less interest in abolition than Friends like Woolman and Anthony Benezet.[42] The behavior of Shrewsbury and Chesterfield meetings supports Frost's conjecture. Shrewsbury Monthly Meeting adopted a stance against slavery earlier than most other local meetings in the Delaware Valley and was concerned greatly about the welfare of blacks. But before 1755 these Friends showed limited interest in disciplining members who married outside the meeting. In contrast, Chesterfield stonewalled on abolitionism until the 1770s and cared little about whether slaves actually obtained liberty; on the other hand, these Quakers consistently punished members who married out even before the Yearly Meeting directive of the mid-1750s.

Tables 8 and 9 clearly illustrate these dissimilarities between the two groups of New Jersey Friends. In the period before 1755—when meetings were not under the watchful eye of the Yearly Meeting on this issue—Shrewsbury was very lenient towards those marrying out. Although the Shrewsbury overseers reported six cases of irregular marriages between 1732 and 1742, no one was disowned, and from 1743 until 1754 the meeting disciplined only one woman, who had married a man too nearly related (see Table 8). That the absence of cases was not the result of the obedient behavior of the Shrewsbury Friends became clear in 1755 when the Philadelphia Yearly Meeting reminded local meetings to enforce the marriage discipline. The Shrewsbury meeting then expressed concern that it was "remiss" in disciplining members who married out and so in 1755 and 1756 the overseers called in twenty-seven Friends who had married out during previous years and requested their acknowledgments. Eighteen of the offenders expressed sorrow for their errors, and their membership was continued. Furthermore, in 1758, the Shrewsbury leaders explained to the Yearly Meeting that they had not visited families because they were "under a sence of [their] Innabillities" to dispense advice to other families when their own families were not in order (7th month). Shrewsbury Friends generally indicated only a mild interest in the enforcement of discipline throughout the period 1732 to 1780. Although the proportion grew to about 40 percent after 1761—largely because Shrewsbury Friends were now enforcing the marriage discipline more strictly—only 34.8 percent of the discipline cases brought into the monthly meeting from 1732 to 1780 ended in disownment (Table 9). In contrast, Chesterfield enforced discipline much more rigidly during the entire period and disowned offenders at a relatively high rate, especially during the 1730s and 1770s. As Table 8 shows, Chesterfield Monthly Meeting consistently disciplined Friends who married out even before the 1755 directive of the Yearly Meeting.[43]

It appears, then, that in their views on both slavery and enforcement of the marriage discipline, Friends from Shrewsbury and Chesterfield drew guidance from two different traditions in interpreting Quaker theology. Shrewsbury Quakers showed little interest in maintaining group coherence by establishing and enforcing rules that drew boundaries between themselves and members of other religions. Instead they demonstrated several of the characteristics of what Max Weber called "exemplary prophecy," which emphasized "the possession of the deity or the inward and contemplative surrender to God." Adherents to this kind of religion *lived* according to God's will, and in this way communicated their ethical standards to others.[44] Thus, the East Jersey Friends after

TABLE 8

ENFORCEMENT OF MARRIAGE DISCIPLINE

	Total Discipline Cases	Marriage Cases (No.)	Marriage Cases (%)
Shrewsbury			
1732–42	9	6	66.7
1743–54	13	1	7.7
Total	22	7	31.8
Chesterfield			
1732–42	22	10	45.4
1743–54	70	45	64.3
Total	92	55	59.8

SOURCES: Shrewsbury and Chesterfield MM minutes, 1732–54.

TABLE 9

DISCIPLINARY CASES

	Total Cases	Cases Ending in Disownment (%)	Marriage Cases[a]	Marriage Cases Ending in Disownment (%)	Slavery Cases[b]	Slavery Cases Ending in Disownment (%)
Shrewsbury						
1732–40	6	16.7	4	0.0	0	
1741–50	10	0.0	2	0.0	0	
1751–60	97	25.8	40	37.5	1	0.0
1761–70	110	40.9	58	53.4	9	55.6
1771–80	128	39.8	51	39.2	5	20.0
Total	351	34.8	155	42.6	15	40.0
Chesterfield						
1732–40	18	55.5	7	57.1	0	
1741–50	37	37.8	28	28.6	0	
1751–60	153	45.8	69	46.4	0	
1761–70	124	37.1	91	36.3	0	
1771–80	245	59.2	117	55.6	15	86.7
Total	577	49.4	312	45.5	15	86.7

SOURCES: Shrewsbury MM minutes, 1732–80; Chesterfield MM minutes, 1732–80.
[a]All cases dealing with marriage, including those involving other offenses.
[b]All cases dealing with slavery, including those involving other offenses.

1725 exhibited their belief that perpetual slavery was a sin by emancipating their own slaves or by not buying any in the first place, rather than by telling others to free theirs. Despite their firm antislavery position, these Quakers sent no petitions to the Yearly Meeting in favor of strengthening the discipline before 1757, as did the Chester meeting, and even in the 1760s and 1770s when slave trading and owning were prohibited, Shrewsbury Friends were more concerned with procuring freedom for the slave than with penalizing the slave trader or owner. In addition, East Jersey Quakers were reluctant to disown members for other kinds of offenses, especially those like marrying out, that violated rules of the Society designed to isolate Friends from people of other religions.

The Chesterfield meeting, on the other hand, tended more to the "emissary type of prophecy" that demands that others follow a prescribed moral code.[45] These Friends were not reluctant to disown wrongdoers, and enforced the marriage discipline consistently before 1755. They were slow in accepting the Yearly Meeting's rules against the slave trade and slavery. In accord with their concern about adhering to the behavioral code rather than to the humanistic spirit of Quakerism, it is likely that Chesterfield leaders assumed a legalistic posture by demanding a sense of the meeting before agreeing that slavery was "wrong." When the Chesterfield meeting did enforce the rules against slavery after 1775, they did so with such speed that they appear to have been more interested in ridding the meeting of slave owners than in obtaining freedom for the blacks involved.

Although Weber assigned all Quakers to his "emissary" category, he did note that their religion "contained very strong contemplative elements" that were common among "exemplary" religions. In fact, Quakerism had characteristics of both types, for as Frost has explained, "one of the reasons why only Friends, of all the sects that sprang up during the Commonwealth period, were able to survive was that they managed to combine the liberty of personal authoritative revelation with a strong system of discipline and church control." The combination of personal revelation and church discipline was not easy to sustain, however, and indeed George Fox found it impossible to convince all of his co-religionists that a system for supervising behavior was necessary. In the 1660s, John Perrot and his adherents had refused to accept a Society ruling that they should take off their hats during worship services. They maintained that they would not force their principles on others, and so they did not want others to tell them how to worship. In the 1670s, John Wilkinson and John Story led a group that denounced new disciplinary procedures and eventually split off from the Society. Both rebelling factions believed that the individual's freedom to communicate with God in his or her own way should not be obstructed by "a tyrannical government."[46]

The authority of the meeting to supervise members' behavior was therefore a question of paramount importance among English Friends in the decades before many of them emigrated to West Jersey and Pennsylvania. It is likely that these Quakers brought with them a concern about the need for such government, but not necessarily any agreement on where to set the balance between discipline and individual conscience. William Penn, in support of Fox, wrote during the Wilkinson-Story controversy that if the meeting did not have discipline "it would be overrun with lukewarm hypocrites and loose walkers."[47] His associates who became leaders of the Chesterfield meeting probably agreed.

Quakers in Shrewsbury had not experienced this turmoil, and thus were less concerned about discipline. Many of them were among a number of people with Anabaptist and Seeker leanings who had emigrated to Long Island from Lynn, Massachusetts, during the 1640s. They had converted to Quakerism after missionaries arrived in New Netherland in 1657, but kept close ties with their Baptist neighbors—some of whom protected them from persecution and migrated with them to East Jersey. Shrewsbury Friends did not set up monthly meetings for discipline on their own in the 1660s, but created them only when George Fox visited in 1672 to encourage Friends there to establish these meetings.[48] The very different past experiences of the Shrewsbury Friends, then, and especially their unusually favorable association with members of other religions, made them less interested in devising a disciplinary system that would erect boundaries between themselves and other groups.

By the mid-eighteenth century, then, Shrewsbury and Chesterfield Friends had fundamentally different points of view on how Quakers should practice their beliefs, which continued to guide their behavior when slavery became an issue. They emphasized separate strands of Quaker tradition, and so had divergent ideas about the identity of Friends within society. The difference between the Shrewsbury and Chesterfield meetings sprang primarily from their different local experiences with the institution of slavery, though their dissimilar views on the fundamentals of Quakerism also played a part.

Like Quakers elsewhere, members of the Shrewsbury meeting did not at first recognize that slavery conflicted with their ideals. Comparatively few blacks lived in Monmouth County before 1710, and slaves were viewed primarily as a source of labor. With the New York slave rebellion of 1712 and the huge increase of blacks imported into the Shrewsbury area after 1710, however, Friends had to face up to the fact that slavery violated their beliefs. A system of perpetual bondage necessitated the use or threat of violence within families and by society, and it contradicted the belief that all men and women were equal in the eyes of God. And slave ownership, as John Hepburn pointed out so well, encouraged pride and sloth.

The Shrewsbury Quaker slave owners of the early eighteenth century, needing help in developing and exploiting their plantations, used Afro-Americans, who were the most readily available source of labor in their locality. Thus, while they manumitted their slaves in response to the urgings of Hepburn, traveling ministers like John Salkield, and their own consciences, they did so only after obtaining the benefits of slave ownership.[49] But even though these early emancipators put off proclaiming their disapproval of perpetual servitude until they were near death, and deprived their children but not themselves of the slaves' labor, they did establish a precedent for the gradual elimination of slavery that was followed by most members of the Shrewsbury meeting after 1730. Many

Friends living in eastern Monmouth County after 1750 avoided owning slaves both because they did not need additional labor and because they thought Quakers could practice their religious ideals by so doing. Then at mid-century when the issue of slavery busied the Yearly Meeting, the Shrewsbury meeting retained the "exemplary" style of the earlier generation by placing more emphasis on obtaining freedom for blacks than on punishing the wrongdoers.

In contrast and in order to maintain a separate identity in West Jersey society, Chesterfield Friends relied more heavily on meeting discipline, particularly in controlling marriage, than on individual commitment to the Quaker ideals that underlay antislavery. Slavery was relatively unimportant in the Burlington County area until after 1740, and, as in Shrewsbury before 1710, was not considered a danger to the integrity of the Quaker community. During the 1750s and 1760s, some Chesterfield leaders were concerned about the growth of slavery in their locality, but many others relied on slave labor to run their farms, and were reluctant to stop buying Afro-Americans or to free their slaves. When Chesterfield finally reached a sense of the meeting in favor of antislavery in the mid-1770s after most of its slave-owning leaders had died, moved away, or otherwise left positions of power, the meeting acted in a way that was consistent with its past disciplinary policy. The weighty Chesterfield Friends worked vigorously to rid the meeting of slaveholders, with little regard for the consequences of that policy for the freedom of blacks. Whereas the Shrewsbury meeting patiently worked for and required the manumission of all slaves its members bought, sold, owned, or hired from non-Quakers, the Chesterfield meeting limited its policy to the abrupt disownment of recalcitrant slave owners.

Notes

1. For a discussion of this literature, see Jean Ruth Soderlund, "Conscience, Interest, and Power: The Development of Quaker Opposition to Slavery in the Delaware Valley, 1688–1780" (Ph.D. diss., Temple University, 1982), pp. 24–37.

2. John E. Pomfret, *The Province of East New Jersey, 1609–1702* (Princeton: Princeton University Press, 1962), pp. 42–45; Peter O. Wacker, *Land and People: A Cultural Geography of Preindustrial New Jersey: Origins and Settlement Patterns* (New Brunswick, N.J.: Rutgers University Press, 1975), p. 130; Norman H. Maring, *Baptists in New Jersey; A Study in Transition* (Valley Forge, Pa.: The Judson Press, 1964), p. 13; *The Journal of George Fox*, ed. Norman Penney (Cambridge, England: Cambridge University Press, 1911), 2:226.

3. *Journal of George Fox* 2:226.

4. Ibid.; Thomas Jefferson Wertenbaker, *The Founding of American Civilization: The Middle Colonies* (New York: Cooper Square Publishers, Inc., 1963), p. 124; Pomfret, *East New Jersey*, p. 46; "Tables of the Sittings of the Provincial Assemblies, with the Names

of the Members," *Proceedings of the New Jersey Historical Society* 5 (1850): 19–33; Donald L. Kemmerer, *Path to Freedom: The Struggle for Self-Government in Colonial New Jersey, 1703–1776* (Cos Cob, Conn.: John E. Edwards, Publisher, 1968), p. 358; Wacker, *Land and People*, p. 168; Ned Landsman, "Scottish Communities in the Old and New Worlds, 1680–1760" (Ph.D. diss., University of Pennsylvania, 1979), chap. 5.

5. The information in Tables 1, 3, 5, and 6 of this paper came from the analysis of all extant probate records for the New Jersey areas in which most Shrewsbury and Chesterfield Monthly Meeting members lived. The New Jersey probate records are located in the State of New Jersey's Division of Archives and Records Management, Trenton. The samples used in these tables are selected by time and bounded by geographic area. Two periods—1730–39 and approximately 1765 to 1780—are studied because they yield information concerning the economic activities and slaveholding of Friends and their neighbors during or immediately following the times when the positions on slavery of the two monthly meetings are known (1730 and 1756–1780).

The probate records and tax lists of Shrewsbury and Middletown townships were chosen for study because almost all Shrewsbury MM members lived in those two townships. In fact, most lived in Shrewsbury. In the Chesterfield area, the inclusion of all townships where Friends lived was difficult because, although most lived in Burlington County, a few lived in four other counties as well. The small number of Friends living in Somerset, western Middlesex, and Hunterdon counties did not seem to warrant extensive analysis of these localities. Therefore, the samples of all extant probate records for Chesterfield MM include only the five townships in Burlington County where most Chesterfield Friends lived (Chesterfield, Nottingham, Mansfield, New Hanover, and Springfield townships) and Upper Freehold Township in Monmouth County.

It is important to note here that study of probate records reveals slave ownership at the decedents' deaths and may not typify slaveholding patterns in a locality or a meeting at any given time. Thus, these data from inventories may exaggerate the importance of slavery because older residents were able to accumulate the capital to buy slaves; but they may also underestimate slaveholding if masters gave away or sold their black laborers before their death. Still, these probate records are the only way here, as in many historical contexts where good tax series are absent, to study changes in property over time.

6. Sources of Quaker meeting records for both the Shrewsbury and Chesterfield MM areas include Shrewsbury MM minutes, 1732–80; Shrewsbury Quarterly Meeting minutes, 1705–80; Shrewsbury MM Birth, Death, and Marriage records, 1657–1780; Philadelphia Yearly Meeting minutes, 1681–1780; Chesterfield MM minutes, 1684–1783; Chesterfield MM Birth, Death, and Marriage records, 1659–1780; Chesterfield MM Manumissions, 1774–96; Burlington MM minutes, 1681–1780; Burlington MM Birth, Death, and Marriage records, 1678–1780; all located in Friends Historical Library, Swarthmore College. Sources of church records for the area include First Reformed Church of Freehold and Middletown (Marlboro, N.J.), Book of Baptisms, Marriages, Officers, and Communicants, 1709–80, trans. and published in *Genealogical Magazine of New Jersey*, Vols. 22–26, 31–32, 35; Old Tennent Presbyterian Church, Freehold, N.J., Records of Pastors, Officers, Subscribers, Communicants, Baptisms, and Burials, 1706–80, published in Frank R. Symmes, *History of the Old Tennent Church*, 2nd ed. (Cranbury, N.J.: George W. Burroughs, 1904), pp. 175–359; Christ Church, Shrewsbury, Parish Register, 1733–80, published in John E. Stillwell, *Historical and Genealogical Miscellany*, 5 vols., (New York: privately published, 1903–32), 1:157–219; Baptist Church, Middletown, N.J., Records, 1712–80, published in Stillwell, *Miscellany* 2:256–62; James Mott's Journal (Book of Church Discipline, Middletown Baptist Church), 1748–77, published in Stillwell, *Miscellany* 2:263–75; St. Mary's Church, Burlington, N.J., Parish Register, 1703–80, published in Stillwell, *Miscellany* 2:49–133.

7. Wertenbaker, *Middle Colonies*, p. 124; Pomfret, *East New Jersey*, p. 44; Sarah Reape, 58–63M, Monmouth County Wills.

8. Participants in the monthly meetings, whom I also refer to as "leaders," were all Friends who were appointed to offices (such as clerk of meeting or treasurer), or committees (to investigate the behavior of Friends, etc.). In the sample of early Shrewsbury MM participants (those active before 1732), all were important leaders because only the rep-

resentatives to the Yearly and Shrewsbury QM are known. There are no extant minutes of the monthly meeting before 1732.

The sample of probate records used for tables dealing with meeting leadership is different from the samples of all extant probate records for the periods 1715–39 and 1764–80. The wills and inventories of all Shrewsbury and Chesterfield MM participants who died before 1781 and who lived in any township in the meeting areas have been analyzed regardless of year of death. For those participants who did not die by 1780, the tax lists of 1774 and 1778–79 for the entire meeting areas have been utilized.

9. Soderlund, "Conscience, Interest, and Power," pp. 172–73, 191–93; Evarts B. Greene and Virginia D. Harrington, *American Population Before the Federal Census of 1790* (New York: Columbia University Press, 1932), p. 110.

10. John Hepburn, *The American Defence of the Christian Golden Rule, or an Essay to Prove the Unlawfulness of Making Slaves of Men* ([New York?], 1715), pp. 1–2, 12–25.

11. Ibid., pp. 3–6.

12. Philadelphia YM minutes, 19–28/7M/1730.

13. Simeon F. Moss, "The Persistence of Slavery and Involuntary Servitude in a Free State (1685–1866)," *Journal of Negro History* 35 (July, 1950):300. The value of his analysis is limited because blacks mentioned in wills and inventories themselves were not always listed in the abstracts printed in the *New Jersey Archives*. Moss did not investigate the religion of the emancipators; Elias Mestayer, 457M, Monmouth County Wills.

14. John Lippincott, 111M, Joseph Wardell, 649–51M, George Williams, Sr., 1193–97M, 1853–59M, John Lippincott, 1413–14M, 1537M, Thomas White, Sr., 1457–62M, Walter Harbert, 2075–80M, Monmouth County Wills.

15. *The Journal and Major Essays of John Woolman*, ed. Phillips P. Moulton (New York: Oxford University Press, 1971), p. 152.

16. Samuel Nevill, comp. *The Acts of the General Assembly of the Province of New Jersey 1703–1752* (Philadelphia: William Bradford, 1752), pp. 23–24.

17. William Woolley, 3753–55M and Catherine Hartshorne, 3329–31M, Monmouth County Wills; the wills of Shrewsbury MM participants who died in the period between 1757 and 1760 indicate that the Philadelphia YM and Shrewsbury QM decisions of 1755–57 to discipline slave traders had not had immediate effect. Two of eight decedents (25 percent) in this group owned slaves—only slightly less than the percentage for the entire period 1741–60. Joanna Eaton, 3666–67M, Monmouth County Wills. The man had to pay Eaton's daughter 40 shillings per year.

18. Shrewsbury QM minutes, 25/7M/1757; Philadelphia YM minutes, 23–29/9M/1758; minutes of all quarterly meetings of the YM.

19. Shrewsbury MM minutes, 7/6M/1762, 5/11M/1764, 4/3M/1765. See Soderlund, "Conscience, Interest, and Power," chap. 2. From the early 1760s, Wilmington MM also required freedom for blacks who were bought and sold.

20. Shrewsbury MM minutes, 7M/1770, 8M/1770, 1M to 4M/1772, 1M/1773 to 2M/1774.

21. Shrewsbury MM minutes, 7/8M/1775.

22. John Corlies, 2443–46M, Monmouth County Wills; Corlies died in 1760. Shrewsbury MM minutes, 1/7M/1776, 4M/1778, 12M/1778, 10M/1780.

23. The economic variations do describe differences between the groups that may have influenced their attitudes toward slavery, however.

The tax rateables lists are located in the Division of Archives and Records Management. Few exist for the years before 1774. The first year for which lists survive for most townships in the Shrewsbury and Chesterfield meeting areas is 1779. The lists used were: for the Shrewsbury MM, Shrewsbury Township 1779 and Middletown Township 1779; for the Chesterfield MM, Chesterfield Township 1779, Mansfield Township 1779, New Hanover Township 1779, Nottingham Township 1779, and Springfield Township 1779 in Burlington County, and Upper Freehold Township 1778 (none exists for 1779) in Monmouth County.

The value that took into account the total assessed wealth of taxpayers varied from one tax list to another. Some listed the amount of tax to be paid, while others indicated a "rate" from which the actual tax was calculated. In order to compare mean wealth in these different townships, I have computed the value of assessed property by determining the ratio of tax or rates on each tax list to the value of assessed property. Upper Freehold is not included in the discussion of mean wealth because different assessment methods and rates were used there in the two years. The wide gap between mean assessments in East and West Jersey that is evident in Table 4 suggests that different methods might have been used in the two areas. The tax assessments in both places were governed by the same provincial laws, however, and the same rates were assigned to livestock. Therefore, the variation probably arose from real differences in wealth based on the differences in landholdings.

I have not converted these assessment values from provincial currency into pounds sterling because John T. McCusker's tables end in 1775, and I have no idea by how much these rates may be inflated. John J. McCusker, *Money and Exchange in Europe and America, 1600–1775: A Handbook* (Chapel Hill: University of North Carolina Press, 1978).

24. Officers included clerks, treasurers, overseers, ministers, and elders.

25. Shrewsbury MM minutes, 1732–80. Robert Hartshorne and Richard Lawrence were members of the New Jersey Assembly. Lawrence in 1761 and 1762 supported bills laying importation duties on slaves, including one bill that would have been prohibitive had it passed. In 1775 he supported an easier manumission law that did not pass. I am indebted to Thomas L. Purvis for this information.

26. *Journal of John Woolman*, p. 27, and pp. 23–192 *passim.*

27. Wacker, *Land and People*, pp. 126, 159, 178, 184; "Table of the Sittings of the Provincial Assemblies," 19–33; Kemmerer, *Path to Freedom*, p. 358; Ewan M. Woodward and John F. Hageman, *History of Burlington and Mercer Counties, New Jersey* (Philadelphia: Everts and Peck, 1883), includes civil lists for townships in Burlington County. Those townships in the Chesterfield meeting area for which colonial records exist are Chesterfield, 1700–1882 (pp. 280–83); Mansfield, 1773–1882 (p. 354); and Springfield, 1776–1882 (pp. 441–42).

28. See note 5 for a description of the geographic area included in this study; Franklin Ellis, *History of Monmouth County, New Jersey* (Philadelphia: R. T. Peck and Co., 1885), p. 623.

29. See Soderlund, "Conscience, Interest, and Power," pp. 190–204.

30. The sample of meeting participants is different in Chesterfield than in Shrewsbury during the period before 1732 because all the minutes survive in Chesterfield; thus men who played smaller roles in this meeting are also included; William Cooke, 6613–16C (man freed in 1760 by heirs), Benjamin Shreve, 4861–66C (man freed in 1751 but was to pay 40 shillings per year for five years for old age), Daniel Doughty, 10569C (freed old man at death in 1778), William Wood, 10729C, Burlington County Wills; Chesterfield MM Manumissions, 1777 (Wood manumitted slave children before his death in 1778); Matthew Watson freed slaves before his death in 1750, Burlington County Abolition Society Papers, Burlington County Historical Society.

31. Chesterfield MM minutes, 3M/1730; (Thomas Lambert owned five slaves when he died in 1733, and Isaac Horner owned at least two in 1760) Thomas Lambert, 2373–82C, Isaac Horner, 7081–84C, Burlington County Wills; Chesterfield MM minutes, 6/6M/1730.

32. Chesterfield MM minutes, 4/5M/1758, 11M/1758, 1/2M/1759, 7/8M/1760, 6/8M/1761, 4/2M/1762, 5/8M/1762, 3/2M/1763, 2/8M/1764, 7/8M/1766, 6/8M/1767, 3M/1771 to 5M/1771, 6/8M/1772, 3/8M/1775.

33. Chesterfield MM manumissions, 1774; Dury left her personal property (£26.9 sterling) to four other blacks when she died in 1783, see Mary Dury, 1201J, Hunterdon County Wills; Chesterfield MM minutes, 1/8M/1776, 2/2M/1776, 7/3M/1776.

34. Chesterfield MM manumissions, 1777–78; Chesterfield MM minutes, 10/9M/1778, 3/12M/1778, 4/3M/1779, 8M/1779, 11M/1779; Chesterfield MM manumissions, 1779–80; Chesterfield MM minutes, 6/5M/1779, 5/8M/1779, 11M/1779, 5M/1780, 10M/1780.

35. Chesterfield MM minutes, 5/8M/1779, 8M/1780, 8M/1781, 8M/1782; Chesterfield MM manumissions, 1781–83; Chesterfield MM minutes, 5M/1783; Chesterfield MM manumissions, 1786–97; Chesterfield MM minutes, 1754–83.

36. Isaac Horner, 7081–84C, John Newbold, 8555C, William Pancoast, 7517–24C, Timothy Abbott, 10062–75C, William Cooke, 6613–16C, Isaac Forman, 9654C, Burlington County Wills; Gideon Bickerdike, 557J, Hunterdon County Wills; Eliakim Hedger, Book

12, 470, Somerset County Wills; Chesterfield MM minutes, 1730–1776; Daniel Doughty, 10569C, Burlington County Wills; for Morris, see the Manumission Book of the Three Philadelphia MMs, 1774.

37. Samuel Worth and Joseph Horner, Chesterfield MM manumissions, 1777; Chesterfield MM manumissions, Thomas Thorn 1779, Samuel Olden 1777, Robert White and William Clarke, 1779; Chesterfield MM minutes, 1770–83; Chesterfield MM manumissions, 1779.

38. Chesterfield MM minutes, 1745–83.

39. Philadelphia YM minutes, 23–29/9M/1758; Mathew Champion, Lib. 4, 38, John Sykes, 9059C, William Cooke, 6613–16C, Burlington County Wills; Report of the Committee on James McCarty's Estate, 17/9M/1770, Burlington County Abolition Society Papers, BCHS.

40. See note 23.

41. Robert Barclay, *An Apology for the True Christian Divinity. . . .* ([London] 1678), prop. 15, arts. 13–15; Herbert Aptheker, *American Negro Slave Revolts* (New York: International Publishers, 1974), pp. 162–208. Aptheker has been criticized for including many rumored conspiracies and individual or small group acts of violence that cannot be considered actual slave revolts, but his examination in Chapter 2 of how rumors of rebellion—both real and imaginary—aroused fears among whites is very important; several Friends who manumitted their slaves in their wills, as mentioned above, used freedom as a reward for correct behavior by including the restriction that the slaves would not be freed in the future unless they behaved themselves in the meantime. For example, George Williams, Sr., 1193–97M, 1853–59M and John Lippincott (II), 1413–14M, 1537M, Monmouth County Wills.

42. J. William Frost, "The Origins of the Quaker Crusade Against Slavery: A Review of Recent Literature," *Quaker History* 67 (Spring 1978):56–58; Frederick B. Tolles, *Meeting House and Counting House: The Quaker Merchants of Colonial Philadelphia, 1682–1763* (Chapel Hill: University of North Carolina Press, 1948), chap. 10.

43. Shrewsbury MM minutes, 1732–80; Chesterfield MM minutes, 1684–1780.

44. Max Weber, "The Social Psychology of the World Religions," in *From Max Weber: Essays in Sociology*, trans. and ed. H. H. Gerth and C. Wright Mills (New York: Oxford University Press, 1958), p. 285.

45. Ibid.

46. Ibid., 291; J. William Frost, *The Quaker Family in Colonial America* (New York: St. Martin's Press, 1973), p. 48–49; William C. Braithwaite, *The Second Period of Quakerism*, ed. Henry C. Cadbury, 2nd ed. (Cambridge, England: Cambridge University Press, 1961), pp. 228–36, 291–97. The Hutchinsonian and Half-Way Covenant crises among New England Puritans in the 1630s and 1660s contained similar tensions, of course.

47. Braithwaite, *Second Period*, p. 299.

48. Rufus M. Jones, *The Quakers in the American Colonies* (London: MacMillan & Co., Ltd., 1911), pp. 216–23; Pomfret, *East New Jersey*, pp. 42–45; *Journal of George Fox* 2:226; Frederick B. Tolles, "The Atlantic Community of the Early Friends," Supplement no. 24, *The Journal of the Friends' Historical Society* (1952):23.

49. John Hepburn mentioned that Salkield spoke against slavery (*American Defence*, p. 3). Salkield was a traveling minister who emigrated from England to Chester, Pennsylvania in 1705. He probably visited Shrewsbury on at least one of his journeys between Pennsylvania and New England in 1701, 1702, or 1708–09. See Society of Friends, Philadelphia Yearly Meeting, *Quaker Biographical Sketches of Ministers and Elders . . . 1682–1800*, ed. Willard C. Heiss (Indianapolis, 1972), pp. 255–58.

Conflict, Community and Religious Affiliation in Colonial New Jersey

Douglas Jacobsen

Douglas Jacobsen is an assistant professor of church history at Messiah College in Grantham, Pennsylvania. He is working on a general history of religion in colonial America.

IN CONTRAST to most of the papers that are being presented today, I would like to broach a broader topic, one that addresses the overall structure of religion in colonial New Jersey. As a means of introducing the general subject of religion in the colony, let me recount a conversation held in 1751 between the itinerant Lutheran minister Henry Melchior Muhlenberg and a member of the New Jersey Assembly. The two met on the road that connected the Hudson crossing from New York with Hackensack, and as they traveled together the subject of religion naturally arose. Muhlenberg records the conversation in his journal.

> The assembleeman . . . said that there was no unity at all among the preachers and they ought, after all, to set a good example to others. I told him that he was asking for the impossible; there could be no fellowship between Christ and Belial, between light and darkness, and righteousness and unrighteousness could have no part in each other . . . He admitted that I was right and began to speak of other things.[1]

The "assembleeman" who engaged Muhlenberg in conversation was baffled by the complexity of religion in the colony. Everywhere he looked, conflict and disarray seemed to be the order of things. In his own understanding of the matter, religion should have an opposite effect, that of fostering community. Religion was not performing that role in society, and the assemblyman thought the preachers of the colony were to blame.

Muhlenberg had a wholly different appraisal of the situation. He argued that it was not the purpose of religion to promote the unity of society. Religion was concerned with truth, not the unity of society. In the process of revealing the truth, religion naturally and necessarily spawned conflict and divisions within society. Divisions of religious affiliation could not and should not be eradicated—they were the only means of visibly separating truth from heresy.

In the above conversation, three basic issues were raised and two opinions were expressed. The three issues can be identified by the terms *conflict*, *community* and *religious affiliation*. The two opinions represent different weightings of the relative importance of each of these in the religious structure of the colony. The discussion began with the assemblyman's tentative assertion of the need for community and ended with Muhlenberg's pointed explication of the realities of conflict and religious affiliation.

Though over two centuries separate us from these events, present scholarship reflects an awareness of issues and weighting of opinion very similar to that of Muhlenberg and his partner in conversation. Themes of conflict and religious affiliation have dominated recent historiography concerning religion in colonial New Jersey, while the reality of community often has been disparaged. In contrast to this pattern, I would like to resurrect the assemblyman's concern. I see a need to establish the importance of another element, along with conflict and religious affiliation, in the structure of religion in colonial New Jersey. That element is a religiously grounded sense of community. I have no desire to underrate conflict and religious affiliation as important components of New Jersey's structure of religion, but I believe that by themselves they provide an insufficiently complex framework for comprehending the whole. In order to do justice to the actual complexity of New Jersey's religious scene, the theme of community must be raised to a level equal to the other two. In what follows, I would like to sketch out one rendition of this theme.

First, to avoid any possible confusion, let me define my use of the term *community*. When one mentions community, the natural inclination is to think of that close-knit web of personal and emotional face-to-face relations that Ferdinand Tonnies labeled "Gemeinschaft."[2] It is common for us in the modern world to speak of the loss of community. Our fast-paced and technological environment is seen as antithetical to real community, which needs time and personal involvement to develop. This is not what I intend by the term *community*.

My concern is with social community. Plato defined community as "a having-in-common of pleasures and pain."[3] Following Plato, social community can be described as those ideals, beliefs, and values that the members of a society hold together. Ideas held in common eventually hold together, and taken in this sense, social community represents the glue of society—the central ideas that hold the society together.

In colonial New Jersey, social community was religious in two ways. First, social community was religious in the traditional sense of the term. Because the great majority of the colony's inhabitants were Protestant Christians, it was natural that the language of Protestant Christianity should come to provide the rhetorical symbols through which social community was expressed. Despite the fact that Jerseyans heartily and consistently rejected the formal institutionalization of any religious establishment, they always conceived of their society as a Christian society.

Secondly, social community in New Jersey can be conceived as religious by definition. Social community is not a mere aggregation of interests; rather, it reflects a deeply felt allegiance to what that society takes to be the irreducibly real. It represents what Emile Durkheim labeled the noncontractual element in all social contracts. The irreducibility of this focused center of social community has led many sociologists to brand the phenomenon as functionally equivalent to religion. Edward Shils, to cite one person, has remarked, "In this sense, every society has an 'official' religion, even when that society or its exponents and interpreters conceive of it, more or less correctly, as a secular, pluralistic, and tolerant society."[4]

It is important to keep these two ways of understanding the "religiousness" of social community in mind as we look at the history of the phenomenon in the colony. While the two are not necessarily mutually exclusive—the first represents a specifically Christian adaptation of the second, more functional definition—their different emphases can help to organize the historical data. Seen in this light, the history of the idea of community in colonial New Jersey divides rather naturally into two slightly overlapping periods.

The first period dates from the founding of the colony roughly to the end of the first decade of the eighteenth century. During this period, Jerseyans experimented with various modifications and applications of old world conceptions of community. In the old world, community had most often been defined as a uniformity of religion. This model of community had originated in the Roman ideal of social order, but the form it had taken immediately antecedent to the founding of New Jersey was that of the national establishment of religion—the state church system.

New Jersey never had an official, state-supported church, but uniformity as the model of community persisted. This uniformity was rarely sought in religious doctrine. Instead, the history of the colony before the eighteenth century exhibits a consistent sense of the need to define the limits of behavior in line with the moral and ethical sensibilities of the Christian religion. The result of this process can be described as an informal establishment of religion. While no specifically religious arm of the state was ever created, community was still seen as an ideal that needed to be imposed on society, and this ideal was generally conceived in institutional and legal terms.

During the second period, which began in the late 1690s, a new and more flexible conception of community came to the fore. Community was conceived not as an ideal to be imposed on society, but as a reality that simply needed to be recognized as inherent in society. Community was cast in the language of unity rather than the terms of uniformity. While all were not alike and never could be, all should be united for the common good. As the nature of community changed, its locus in society shifted. The idea of community moved out of the legal structure of the colony and increasingly found lodging in the hearts of individual colonists. At the same time, social community severed its ties with organized religion and took on a sacred aura all its own.

Let me illustrate this proposal from the history of the colony. Separation of church and state was a fact of life in New Jersey, but that does not mean that religion had been institutionally removed from the public life of society. Despite the individualistic and liberal terms of the Concessions and Agreements of 1665, concerns for community remained prominent in early New Jersey and often assumed a semiestablishment cast. Philip Carteret, first governor of the colony, expressed the general attitude of the proprietors as well as of many settlers when he convened the first New Jersey Assembly in May 1668. The purpose for calling this assembly into existence was, in the words of Carteret,

> for the making and Constituting such wholsome Lawes as shall be most needfull and Necessary for the good gouernment of the said Prouince, & the maintayning of a religious Communion & ciuil society one wth the other as becometh Christians wthout which it Vmposible for any boddy Politicq to prosper or subsist.[5]

Carteret's purpose was not to establish any church structure; indeed, not one of the laws passed by this assembly dealt directly with the organization or enforcement of religion. Instead, the legislation centered on practical issues, such as licensing and apprenticeship, and, significantly, on moral laws—all of which tied religion and society together on a pragmatic level.

It has sometimes been asserted that these laws have a Puritan hue, having been drawn up and enacted by an assembly that was distinctly New England and Puritan in most of its sentiments. There is some truth to this assertion, but it is a half truth. It is a half truth because it implies that only Puritans would have passed these laws. In actuality, all Englishmen would have basically agreed with the legislation passed in New Jersey, because the English as a whole shared certain assumptions about society and expected those assumptions to be reproduced in the colonies.

By the close of the sixteenth century, most Englishmen had come to believe that God had chosen their nation above all others. Whether Anglican or Puritan, all conceived of their nation as elect in God's sight—preserved and protected throughout history by God's grace. The clearest presentation of this theme can be found in John Foxe's famous sixteenth-century work, the *Actes and Monuments*. In this work he linked a long succession of English rulers who, he claimed, owed their authority directly to God. Foxe attempted to show how these rulers had prospered or failed, depending on whether "they heeded their vocation to defend the faith and the people in the faith."[6] Following Foxe, most Englishmen—with few exceptions—considered it the duty of the sovereign to see that the unique status of England as specially favored by God was maintained. God's favor depended upon the nation's purity, and the law was to enforce that purity. Puritans, Anglicans, and Quakers may have had differing conceptions of purity, but they all agreed that it was the proper principle on which to base society.

The assertion that these basic English assumptions were operating in colonial New Jersey is at odds with the typical presentation of the colony as a free society. Quaker West Jersey in particular has been singled out for its early expressions of religious freedom. For example, Wallace Jamison has called the 1676 Concessions and Agreements of the Quaker West Jersey proprietors "one of the finest statements of religious liberty anywhere."[7] Jamison is correct in one sense, but not in another. The document does indeed include a fine statement of religious liberty, but it must be understood that principles stated are not always principles enforced. The laudatory intonations of the West Jersey Concessions, which asserted that "no men, nor number of men upon earth hath power or authority to rule over men's consciences in religious matters,"[8] must be weighed in balance with laws such as the one passed by the West Jersey Assembly in 1683 which emphasize the desire to maintain the purity of the colony's population. The Assembly stated that

> whereas it hath pleased God to commit this country and Province, into the hands of such who (for the generality of them) are fearing God, and painful and industrious, in the promoting and improving the said Province; and for the better preventing of such as are prophane, loose, and idle, and scandolous from settling amongst us . . . It is therefore hereby enacted by the authority aforesaid, that all person and persons, who shall transport him, or themselves, into this Province, shall within eighteen months after he or they shall arrive in the said Province, procure and produce a certificate under the hands of such of that religious society to whom he or they did belong, or otherwise from two magistrates.[9]

While this document never specifically defines the place of religion in society, it certainly assigns religion a central location. West Jersey wanted as settlers only those who feared God and who could show religious or magisterial certification of that fear. The ungodly—those loose-living and idle individuals—were to be denied entrance to the colony. In New Jersey, Quakers as well as Puritans and Anglicans assumed a relationship joining society and religious uniformity.

By the mid-1680s New Jersey was rapidly becoming an informally established Christian society. While no direct institutional ties existed between the various religious societies and government, numerous laws had been passed that indissolubly tied Christian religious sensibilities to New Jerseyans' expectations of civil comportment and good citizenship. As the proprietary period progressed, laws seem to have become even more explicitly religious in purpose and wording. For example, the West

Jersey Assembly passed a law in 1693 regarding "the Profanation of the Lord's Day." Its preamble reads:

> Whereas it hath been the practice of all societies of Christian professors to set a part one day in the week for the worship and service of God, and that it hath been and is the antient law of England, (according to the practice of primitive Christians) to set a part the first day of the week to that end, and finding by experience that the same good practice and law, hath been greatly neglected in this Province, to the grief of such as profess the Christian religion, and to the scandal thereof. Be it therefore enacted. . . .[10]

While other laws pertaining to the Sabbath had been passed in West Jersey, this particular law is unique in its specific religious warrant.

There is little question that religion and society were linked in the law of the land. Nevertheless, the actual and undeniable religious pluralism of the colony forced Jerseyans to seek some balance between liberty and uniformity in attempts to establish a social community. A good illustration of this quest for balance is provided by the Council of East New Jersey when it considered in 1683 a Sabbath bill that would have required "all p^{r}sons to worship in publick or private or pay 5^{d}."[11]

The council rejected this bill, voicing four specific objections. First, the bill was redundant, since several laws already insured public respect for the Sabbath. Second, it was potentially harmful, because the bill made no provision for distinguishing true from false worship. Third, the bill was unenforceable, and fourth, the council thought the bill simply too fanatical. The observance of the Sabbath was not, in the eyes of the council, a fundamental law of God. In addition to the four specific objections, the council also noted that the proposed bill violated a basic principle of New Jersey life and law. The council felt that the purpose of religious law in East Jersey was to maintain a delicate equilibrium between the extremes of coercing too broad a uniformity of practice or belief and encouraging irreligiousness. Reflecting on the particular bill before them in 1683, the council did not find this proper balance. Their final judgment was that "Lib'ty of Conscience ought to bee p^{r}ferred and Licenciousness punished wch this Bill Seemes not equally to secure." It should be noted that while the reasoning of the council tempers the strictness with which some Jerseyans sought to impose a uniformity of religious practice, it in no way implies a rejection of that uniformitarian ideal.[12]

During the proprietary period, the ideal of maintaining both East and West Jersey as a Christian society was one of the only nongeographical factors that held New Jerseyans together. The informality of this New Jersey "religious establishment" mentality, however, kept it from becoming powerful enough to unite the two colonies into one society. To New

Jerseyans looking for an increased sense of unity and community, the unification of East and West Jersey into one royal colony in 1702 seemed a welcome development. Colonel Robert Quary, for example, wrote to the Lords of Trade in June 1703 stating,

> The Jerseys have been for a long time in confusion, having no Government, which makes them all heartily wish my Lord Cornbury's Commission for that province were come, that so they might be settled on a sure foundation. . . .
>
> . . . It is the expectation of all that His Excellency My Lord Cornbury will reconcile all these differences—unite all interests, settle 'em on a sure foundation—make 'em all easy and happy.[13]

While many New Jerseyans had high hopes of an increased sense of community resulting from Lord Cornbury's arrival as first royal governor, the governor's actual presence soon dashed those hopes. Instead of building a more sure foundation for New Jersey's evolving Christian society, Cornbury's presence threatened to crush the indigenous sense of community beneath the weight of an extremely hierarchical and narrowly instititional religious community ideal. Even though numerous Jerseymen shared Cornbury's basic understanding of community, they disagreed with his application of those principles. Before Cornbury's arrival, a degree of religious uniformity had been sought in moral and ethical matters. For Cornbury, however, doctrinal issues were paramount. At one point he upbraided the assembly:

> I am of opinion that nothing has hindered the Vengeance of just Heaven from falling on this Province long ago, but the infinite Mercy, Goodness, Longsuffering and Forbearance of Almighty God, who has been abundantly provoked by the repeated crying sins of a perverse Generation among us, and more especially by the dangerous and abominable Doctrines, and the wicked Lives and Practices of a number of People, some of whom under the pretended Name of Christians, have dared to deny the very essence and being of the saviour of the World.[14]

Instead of leading to the increased institutionalization of English uniformitarian ideals of community, Cornbury's emphasis seems to have forced Jerseyans to reassess the institutional road of community they had already trod. Except for a handful of bills designed to extend Quaker civil privileges, no further religious or moral legislation was passed by the New Jersey legislature until very late in the colonial period.

Let me relate just one incident that highlights the change of attitude in the colony. In 1721, Governor William Burnet introduced a bill to the assembly of which only the title remains. That title, however, speaks eloquently: "An Act against denying the divinity of our savior Jesus Christ, the doctrine of the blessed trinity, the truth of the holy scriptures and spreading atheistical books."[15] At first blush, this bill with its doctrinal emphasis seems wholly out of line with any New Jersey sense of community. If it seems out of place to us, it also seemed so to the assembly. On its second reading the bill was summarily dropped from the house agenda. The Baptist minister and assemblyman Nathaniel Jenkins spoke for many when he stated, "I believe the doctrines in question as firmly as the promoters of that ill-designed bill; but will never consent to oppose the opposers with law; or with any other weapon, save that of argument."[16] Samuel Smith, the Quaker historian, offered the assessment that "assemblies in the colonies have rarely troubled themselves with these subjects, perhaps never before or since."[17]

While it is easy to laud the assembly for its libertarian magnanimity, it must be pointed out that the historical consciousness of these legislators seems somewhat defective. Only twenty-five years earlier, for example, the West Jersey Assembly had passed a bill which contained the same essential contents as the bill defeated in 1721. An act of 1696 demanded that before anyone could hold any public office in the colony he must profess "faith in God the Father, and in Jesus Christ, his eternal Son the true God, and in the Holy Spirit one God blessed for ever more; and . . . acknowledge the Holy Scriptures of the Old and New Testament, to be given by Divine inspiration."[18]

The philosopher Ernest Gellner refers to certain historical developments as "humps of transition."[19] Human history does not progress on a flat plane, he says, but rather traverses an undulating surface of reality. At each hump of transition, two things happen simultaneously: new vistas of reality appear on the horizon and old conceptions of reality disappear behind the ridge just passed. This type of historical development seems to have taken place in New Jersey between 1696 and 1721. With vision blocked by the recently traversed ridge, the members of the 1721 assembly found it difficult to remember or really understand the situation that had prevailed in the colony only a quarter century before.

Few transitions in history, however, come without some previous indication of the future direction of change, and New Jersey proves no exception. As early as 1698, Governor Jeremiah Basse had perceived the need for a new community ideal for the colony. In his "Proclamation for the Suppression of Vice and Immorality" issued in that year, Basse announced,

> It being very necessary for the good & prosperity of this Province that our principal care be in obedience to the laws of God & the wholesome laws of this Province to endeavor as much as in us lyeth the exterpation of all sorts of looseness & prophanitie & to unite & Join in the fear & love of God & of one another that by the religious and vertuous carriage & behavior of every one in his

> respective station & calling all heats & animosities & dissentions may vanish, & the blessing of Almighty God accompany our honest & lawfull endeavors.[20]

Basse believed that legislation was no longer sufficient to insure "the maintayning of a religious Communion and ciuil society one with the other" referred to in Carteret's earlier address to the assembly.[21] The new theme announced by Basse was that "all heats and animosities and dissentions" should vanish. An emotional joining together in the love as well as the fear of God was necessary to insure that the colony would prosper.

By 1716, Basse had refined his thoughts. No longer governor, Assemblyman Basse sermonized on the subject in a speech delivered to the assembly on January 15 of that year.

> Would to God, Mr. Speaker, we could each of us learn to look upon another to be better than himself; to let that charity, which is the golden bond that connects heaven and earth together, . . . govern both our lives and actions. We complain, Mr. Speaker, of bad crops, blasts, mildews, and sometimes of epidemical distempers raging among us. It is no wonder if our common Parent sends these scourges, that by these means he might teach us to love one another. . . . Let us unite in love, and then, how inexpressibly beautiful would such a union be?[22]

In 1698 Basse had stressed the need to augment "wholesome laws" with a corporate joining "in the fear and love of God." By the time of the later address, legal tactics designed to promote community had been dropped altogether. Community still needed to be encouraged, but it appears that Basse would have agreed with the Baptist Jenkins's assertion that it should make its way with no "other weapon, save that of argument." Community, for Basse, was a primal and prereligious human reality that existed whether recognized or not: a "common parent" (i.e., God) sought to teach Jerseyans to love each other. Basse's injunction was not that all Jerseyans should become brothers by acting alike, but that they should act as the brothers they in fact already were.

Basse's speech was not an isolated phenomenon; the same theme was soon resonating throughout the entire spectrum of New Jersey society. One sphere of society which quickly displayed the attitude was the specifically religious realm. As early as 1725 the Presbyterian minister Joseph Morgan wrote in *The Duty and Mark of Zion's Children* that "when instead of Praying for Grace, men Pray against each other. . . . It is time for Zion's Children to Mourn and Weep."[23] In this quotation, Basse's injunction to love each other is converted into the negative—don't pray against each other—but Morgan's work later contains positive instructions toward strengthening community. "Beg of him to pity your Neighbors who know no need of pity from any, and desire none to help them, and think to deal honestly with their Neighbors, is enough to save them."[24]

As New Jersey's new sense of community developed, more was demanded than just getting along, more than the mere absence of conflict. For Morgan, neighborliness could not be a passive virtue. Indicative of the direction of development is another tract published by Morgan in 1732. Entitled *The Nature of Riches*, the work argued that economic practices should be dictated by a brotherly-neighborly ideal of community. Morgan believed God had so structured the world that cooperation was unavoidable. He wrote,

> Riches are given for Publick Good, and it is not in the Skill of the most covetous and envious Man to make it otherwise. It must be put to the use it was made for. He cannot swallow it all into his own Belly. Others must have a part with him, or he cannot gain or keep his Riches.[25]

Morgan, like Basse, believed that God, independent of any specifically religious means, had woven a brotherhood into the very essence of society. Recognition of this brotherhood would spur individuals on to act in accordance with their own best interests and the interests of the "Publick Good."

The idea of society as an interdependent and interpersonal organization—a neighborly network instituted by God—was quickly adopted by most Jerseyans. As the colonial era progressed, a neighborly and egalitarian ideal of community slowly spread. Foreign visitors noticed the distinctive social milieu of the colony. Nicholas Collins, for one, wrote home to Sweden in 1771 saying, "Here in New Jersey almost everyone is of the same stamp. Many a one goes and ploughs who is owner of one or two hundred thousand dollars. All are called gentlemen and ladies."[26]

In addition to foreign accounts, the real proof of New Jersey's religious community pudding is found in the metamorphosis of individuals and groups that had grown and matured in the colony. Let me recount just one example of change in an individual that illustrates the depth of change in the colony. In his young adult years, Lewis Morris had been an Anglican zealot. As governor of the colony, he had worn the visage of a self-proclaimed enlightened despot. But by the time of his death a new strain of personality was evident. Apparently Morris was not immune to the effects of New Jersey's atmosphere of brotherhood and in his crotchety way he finally acceded to it. His will reads in part:

> I forbid . . . any man to be paid for preaching a funeral sermon over me: Those who survive me, will commend or blame my conduct in

> life as they think fit, and I am not for paying of any man for doing of either; but if any man, whether churchman or dissenter, in or not in priests's orders, is inclined to say anything on that occasion, he may, if my executors think fit to admit him to do it.[27]

For a final evaluation of his life Morris did not turn to the church of his youth—the church he had once desired to see established as the religion of the colony. Rather he sought the unsolicited judgments of his neighbors. In doing so, he affirmed that in mid-eighteenth-century New Jersey, few other evaluations were as important. New Jersey's community ideal seems indeed to have taken on a religious significance of its own.

The foregoing has obviously not been an exhaustive treatment of the theme of community as it applies to the study of religion in colonial New Jersey. I hope, however, that this cursory treatment has indicated the importance of the phenomenon. Let me note just two specific ways in which an awareness of the religious importance of social community might alter present understandings of religion in the colony—understandings that have largely developed around themes of conflict and religious affiliation.

First, I would suggest that most studies of religion in New Jersey have been too narrowly conceived. A recognition of the religious dimension of society as social community should broaden future approaches.

Second, the theme of community can help explain the reason why religious toleration blossomed in the colony as the eighteenth century progressed. One scholar has suggested that the "close association of different religious traditions led inevitably to a 'live and let live' attitude on the part of the laity which the sectarianism of the clergy was never able to eradicate."[28] For my part, I fail to see either the inevitability of this result or the adamant opposition of the clergy. Toleration did not develop without a rationale or necessarily from the ground up. Rather, clergy and laity, together with the public leaders of the colony, were all participant-observers in the development of a public and religious community ideal that not only allowed, but fostered, mutual toleration and respect.

Notes

1. Henry Melchior Muhlenberg, *The Journals of Henry Melchior Muhlenberg*, trans. Theodore Tuppert and John W. Doberstein (Philadelphia: The Evangelical Lutheran Ministerium of Pennsylvania and Adjacent States, 1942–58), 1:296.
2. Ferdinand Tonnies, *Community and Society* (Gemeinschaft und gesellschaft), trans. and ed. Charles P. Loomis (East Lansing: Michigan State University Press, 1957).

3. Quoted by George E. Gordon Catlin, "The Meaning of Community," in *Community*, ed., Carl J. Friedrich (New York: The Liberal Arts Press, 1959), p. 117.

4. Edward Shils, *Center and Periphery: Essays in Macrosociology* (Chicago: University of Chicago Press, 1975), p. 3.

5. *Archives of the State of New Jersey*, 1st ser. (Newark: New Jersey Historical Society, 1880–93), 1:57. Hereafter *NJA*.

6. William Haller, *Foxe's Book of Martyrs and The Elect Nation* (London: Jonathan Cape, 1963), pp. 224–225.

7. Wallace N. Jamison, *Religion in New Jersey: A Brief History* (Princeton: D. Van Nostrand Co., Inc., 1964), p. 11.

8. Aaron Leaming and Jacob Spicer, *The Grants, Concessions, and Original Constitutions of the Province of New Jersey* (Somerville: Honeyman and Co., 1881), p. 394.

9. Ibid., 474–75.

10. Ibid., 519.

11. *NJA* 13:37.

12. Ibid.

13. Ibid., 2:544.

14. Ibid., 3:182.

15. Samuel Smith, *The History of the Colony of Nova-Caesaria or New Jersey* (1765; reprint, New York: Arno Press, 1962), p. 417.

16. Morgan Edwards, *Materials Toward a History of the Baptists in New Jersey* (Philadelphia: Thomas Dobson, 1792), p. 41.

17. Smith, *Nova-Caesaria*, p. 417.

18. Leaming and Spicer, *Concessions*, p. 549.

19. Ernest Gellner, *Thought and Change* (Chicago: University of Chicago Press, 1964).

20. *NJA* 2:206.

21. *NJA* 1:57.

22. As reported in Richard S. Field, *The Provincial Courts of New Jersey*, Vol. 3 of *Collections of the New Jersey Historical Society* (New York, 1849), pp. 101–2.

23. Joseph Morgan, *The Duty, and a Mark of Zion's Children* (New London, T. Green, 1725), p. 6.

24. Ibid., 18.

25. Joseph Morgan, *The Nature of Riches* (Philadelphia: B. Franklin, 1732), p. 5.

26. *Journal and Biography of Nicholas Collins, 1746–1831,* trans. Amandus Johnson (Philadelphia: The New Jersey Society of Pennsylvania, 1936), p. 27.

27. Smith, *Nova-Caesaria*, p. 434.

28. Jamison, *Religion*, p. 55.

Comments

John F. Wilson

John F. Wilson is the Agate Brown and George L. Collard Professor of Religion at Princeton University. He is the author of *Pulpit in Parliament* and *Public Religion in American Culture,* and a coauthor of *Religion in American History: Interpretive Essays*. He is editing "The Work of Redemption," by Jonathan Edwards.

I AM PLEASED to have the opportunity to comment on these two papers, each of which I think has some very interesting aspects. They diverge so markedly, however, in terms of subject matter, mode of approach, and form of argument that it is a challenge of the first order to treat them together and to suggest useful comparisons between them. For this reason, let me offer comments on each in turn before addressing very briefly what I take to be their point of intersection.

Jean R. Soderlund's discussion of Quaker abolitionism in colonial New Jersey, an analysis developed through comparison between the Shrewsbury and Chesterfield monthly meetings, is a carefully crafted, even an elegant essay. The conventional judgment is that Friends early reached consensus in support of abolition and that they fostered more general support for it. But generalization at that level is often derived from little more than the Quaker espousal of rather nonspecific ideals such as nonviolence, the equality of all folk, and possibly a comparatively simple lifestyle. This paper reaches far deeper and confronts the stubborn fact that the Quaker consensus developed over time, in particular local communities and regions, and according to different schedules. By comparing two monthly meetings, or local communities, of Quakers that manifested different patterns in the development of abolitionist sentiment, Dr. Soderlund has been able to review numerous relevant factors in relationship to the religious factor and also in some measure to isolate that factor and to ask how and in what way or ways it operated. It is no small achievement to set up such a historiographical exercise. What becomes clear from Dr. Soderlund's work is that Quaker religious sentiments operated in relation to numerous other variables.

After paying this tribute to the essay, let me simply share a few questions that occur to me as possible lines of further inquiry. The evidence for a dramatic change of opinion about slaveholding within the Shrewsbury Quaker community against the background of the behavior of the area's non-Quaker population cannot fail to draw attention. While the absolute numbers are very small indeed, the trend, at least among the Quakers of substance, runs directly counter to that among the other inhabitants. We must still ask if we are possibly dealing with generational patterns within the community, but aside from that possibility, the absence of any indication of a power struggle among Quakers is strong presumptive evidence that abolitionist sentiments were significantly at work there. Support for abolitionist sentiments seems to have developed where there was experience with a degree of slaveholding. This social condition clearly came later to Chesterfield in West Jersey than to Shrewsbury in East Jersey. Surely this correlation could be tested by inspecting one or more other local communities where the same kinds of data would be available. Of course, the size of the landholdings in Chesterfield also added a further degree of economic penalty to acting on abolitionist convictions and would need to be taken into account in comparative studies.

If I read Dr. Soderlund's paper correctly, she concludes that the two most important factors in the adoption of abolitionism were socioeconomic circumstances and the development of religious discipline within which Quaker teachings were related to the practices of the meeting's members. This formulation also suggests that comparison with other communities might serve to test the validity of both the framework of analysis and the conclusions.

Further exploration of another avenue of analysis may also be possible. Can more be made of the different origins of these two Quaker communities, one in East and the other West Jersey? Could the New England and Long Island origins of the Shrewsbury group permit comparison with other migrations, possibly to different regions? And did the direct migration from England make a significant cultural difference for Chesterfield and other meetings in parallel communities in Pennsylvania? This is an open question in my mind, for I can imagine that the difference in origin might prove insignificant in relation to the longstanding Quaker involvement with abolitionist convictions. But it is a question that is worth trying to ask and answer.

At the end of the paper Jean Soderlund has recourse to Max Weber's contrast between the emissary or ethical and the exemplary types of prophecy as styles of religious action within societies. In general, she is correct in refusing to accept Weber's dictum that Quakers belong essentially to the emissary or ethical camp and in arguing that the movement may have expressed both styles of social ethic. The different styles might even be linked to the different origins of the two communities noted above. The one style certainly appears in the more direct concern for church government and discipline which the West Jersey Quakers shared with Quakers in the Pennsylvania region. Can this too be tried out in some other relevant case studies?

In sum, Jean Soderlund has demonstrated that there was a religious aspect to the Quaker position on abolition as well as economic, social and political aspects. Imaginative identification and persistent exploration of these matters is itself the best kind of demonstration that religious sensitivities "count," albeit always in social and cultural contexts. That she has skillfully done for us.

Douglas Jacobsen's paper is very different in approach. If I attempted to reduce his argument to a thesis, I think it would take the following form. While generally it has been held that New Jersey stood effectively committed to, indeed was a pioneer in, developing religious liberty and separation between church and state in the New World in the course of the seventeenth century, by the eighteenth century a community had emerged that in fact presupposed a religious valuation of the social order. In Jacobsen's phrase, institutional separation of church and state did not mean that religion had been removed from the public life of society. Here we have a thesis that depends very heavily on a tradition of social theory decisively shaped by Emile Durkheim, the great French sociologist. In Durkheim's view, every collectivity and every community represents itself to itself in essentially religious terms. This has been a powerful idea in anthropology for the interpretation of nonwestern cultures, and increasingly, in the study of classical antiquity. More recently it has been applied to the question of how modern American society might be understood as making behavioral as well as ideological claims upon its members. Douglas Jacobsen has proposed that this kind of model provides a means of interpreting the emergence of New Jersey as a colonial entity that encompassed several religious traditions in a conventional sense while simultaneously uniting them religiously in the different sense suggested by Durkheim.

Now there is no question in my mind that such an interpretation is, at the very least, intriguing. More than this, it has the potential both to suggest new directions for interpreting recognized evidence and to indicate that a greater range of varying kinds of data may have direct relevance to understanding the religious life of a community like colonial New Jersey. Jacobsen makes the case that conventional evidence is at least consistent with what such a Durkheimian model might point to as a possibility. But to make the positive case convincingly along the lines of that model would require surveying a greater range of data. Conceivably such an exercise might support the thesis, undercut it, or even be neutral with respect to it. This we cannot know, however, without going through the process. Let me discuss each of these points in turn.

Douglas Jacobsen has made a case that a residual religious tone in fact continued to inform even those official documents that explicitly provided for the toleration of various religious groups and for religious liberty. What are we to make of this residual religious tone? Was it residual in the language because thought had outpaced expression? Or did it signal a more positive, albeit different, kind of religious attachment in an emerging community? The evidence could be interpreted either way.

For the second point, it is not at all clear from the available data that a decisive new sense of community actually emerged in the late seventeenth and early eighteenth centuries. It may have, but there is little direct evidence in a conventional historiographical sense. The framework Douglas Jacobsen adopts suggests that different kinds of data or evidence might be sought. To use an anthropological approach, religious attachment in an emerging community might be signaled through material culture as much as or even more than through codification in formal public documents or quasi-official explanations embodied in laws, declarations, sermons, tracts, etc. The approach to religion used by the older historiography does not prove very useful on this point. What might be substituted for literary and documentary analysis is a broad and comprehensive review of cultural evidence, however fragmentary, from sources popular as well as high. These materials might range from patterns of town development to architecture, decorative arts, gravestones, burial customs, secular ballads, and festivals and other very important calendrical structures to punctuate time. All this would be grist for the kind of mill that is needed. A systematic canvass and analysis of these kinds of data, incomplete, ambiguous, and evanescent as they are, would take us much closer to answering the question whether a distinctive sense of New Jersey as a community actually emerged early in the eighteenth century. Did this community find expression in a cultural coherence that for want of a better analytical term should be called religious? That is the basic question even if we continue to speak of the separation of religious institutions from developing governmental structures. In this sense, Douglas Jacobsen has set up a remarkably interesting research project. I do not know what kinds or quantities of data actually exist for such an exercise. But I am convinced that an inquiry along these lines would be important and worthwhile. It is at least theoretically possible that a convincing case could be made for the emergence of this new community in colonial New Jersey. So we should thank Douglas Jacobsen for suggesting a most stimulating line of research.

As different as these papers are, there is a link between them. The one is a very tightly controlled and carefully argued analysis of a parallel set of case studies, calculated to illuminate how significant changes of belief and practice came about among the Friends with respect to a central social institution, that of slavery in colonial culture. The other is an attempt to focus on a large and vexing question: what happens to religion in the transition to early modern cultures? Does the substantial and increasing co-residence of positive, religious traditions push all religion to society's margin and secularize the society? Or is this a contemporary judgment we read back into the data? We tend to assume the former. That assumption is myopic because it fails to identify religious expressions of the community that are more inclusive than those compassed by the separate continuing traditions. This is a vast issue, and Douglas Jacobsen has only made the case that an intensive study of the colonial experience of New Jersey focused upon it would be a worthwhile undertaking.

How then are these papers related? Both authors have recognized, although in different ways, that there are important intellectual resources for the study of religion in the literature of social theory. This literature helps us to get a handle on cultural phenomena like religion that are at once so familiar and yet so remote. The emissary/exemplary distinction is just a small element in Max Weber's great studies of the social correlates of the great world religions, while Durkheim's analysis of the necessity of religion to society is a central pillar of his work. Especially when studying cultural subjects like religion, historians have increasingly found it necessary to turn to this kind of literature in order to find new ways of organizing their data. The payoffs demonstrate dramatically the worth of such borrowing and dependence. In very different ways then, these two papers suggest to me how progress in historiography depends upon just such cross-fertilization of disciplines to help us ask old questions in new ways or perhaps even to pose some new questions.

Gilbert Tennent, Revival Workhorse in a Neglected Awakening Theological Tradition

Milton J Coalter, Jr.

Milton J Coalter is the acting director of the Ira J. Taylor Library at the Iliff School of Theology in Denver, Colorado. He is at work on a bibliographic guide to reference resources for American religious history and a history of the Dutch and German Reformed churches.

It is a commonplace observation that the labels given to historical events obscure as much as they reveal. But the obvious bears repeating in the case of the First Great Awakening, since historians have so often overlooked the point. While the first American revival was, as its name suggests, a major colonial happening both in scope and impact, its title misleads when it creates the impression that colonial revivalists were a united group of clergymen with a single theological perspective.

Scholars have tended to picture the mid-eighteenth-century Awakening as a revitalization of New England Puritanism engineered, at least theologically, by that tradition's most ingenious New World offspring, Jonathan Edwards.[1] But the First Great Awakening was greater than colonial Puritanism, New England, or Edwards. Before the quickening of spiritual fervor experienced by Edwards's congregation in Northampton, Massachusetts, "refreshionings of the spirit" erupted in New Jersey under the leadership of the Dutch Reformed clergyman, Theodorus Jacobus Frelinghuysen, and his Presbyterian neighbor, Gilbert Tennent. Both of these men had been deeply influenced by the contemporary thought and practice of continental Reformed Pietists.

Mention of Pietism's influence on colonial American revivalism has been frequent in histories of the period, but serious attention to its content and to its impact on the course of the Awakening has been scant. This oversight has seriously crippled our understanding of the revival experience by eclipsing the fact that Awakeners in the middle colonies were divided among themselves by their varying allegiance to one of two different, although related, Protestant traditions. One of these theological strands was New England Puritanism; the other was continental Pietism.[2]

Several factors can be used to explain historians' neglect of Pietism's contribution to the Awakening, but I will focus on only one, that being what I prefer to call American historiography's "Boston-Jamestown" fetish. On the front cover of the New Yorker some years back, there appeared a rendition of the typical New York resident's image of the United States. The cartoonist reserved a large portion of his canvas for a representation of Manhattan, while the remainder of the country was squeezed into virtual anonymity between New York in the foreground and a land mass in the background labeled California. This New York chauvinism is analogous to the myopia of American historians when they evaluate the relative influences of different segments of the colonial

American population. Until quite recently, colonial historians have tended to look to Massachusetts Bay and Virginia rather than Philadelphia, New Jersey, or New York for the key to what America was and would be in the eighteenth century and beyond. In Awakening historiography specifically, New England has received the lion's share of attention because of Jonathan Edwards's leadership in the region. Edwards has long been recognized as the theological genius of the First Great Awakening and perhaps the most original thinker that America has produced. Edwards's brilliance cannot be disputed. But one can question the penchant of most historians for treating revivalists in the middle colonies and the south as the lackluster stepbrothers of the "fair-haired" boy in the north.

Middle-colony Awakeners in particular deserve more careful study because of the unique characteristics of the revival movement in their region. In New Jersey, New York, Pennsylvania, and Delaware, an unprecedented mixture of ethnic and theological backgrounds among the populace fostered a many-sided conflict, not only between friends and foes of the revivals but also between Pietist and Puritan proponents of new birth.

Participants in this complicated contest did not look to Edwards alone for leadership. Instead, three quite different men acted as role models for the legion of clergymen propagating the call for a new birth in Christ. One was Jonathan Edwards, the second was George Whitefield, and the third was Gilbert Tennent.

Compared to Edwards and Whitefield, Gilbert Tennent has been virtually ignored by Awakening historians. Where his counterparts have been the subjects of innumerable studies, not one publication has examined Tennent's life and thought in depth.[3] This oversight is understandable, at least in part, because Tennent was not as spectacular as the other two. Tennent was not as intellectually agile as Edwards nor as charismatic as Whitefield. He was rather a "workhorse" for the Awakening. The farmer's workhorse is neither as fleet of foot as his master's racehorse nor as stunning in appearance as his stablemate, the show horse. Nevertheless, he was in former times the backbone of the farming enterprise, since his steady labor at the head of a plow prepared the way for the rich harvest that supported his master's kingdom.

This was Gilbert Tennent's role in the Awakening. Tennent was not the theological equal of Edwards or the master of pulpit oratory that George Whitefield was. But he contributed significantly to the Awakening's harvest of souls by traveling more than any other colonial revivalist to defend and preach conversion and practical piety. Moreover, Tennent was the hub of Awakening controversies in the middle colonies during the 1730s and 40s.

Tennent's support of the revival cause may be traced to two men from whom he learned the rudiments of his revival theology and homiletics. The first was his Ulster Scot father and tutor, William Tennent, Sr.; the second, his earliest ministerial colleague, the Dutch Reformed clergyman Theodorus Jacobus Freylinghuysen. From William Tennent, Gilbert acquired an abiding distaste for Christian rationalists who stressed theological orthodoxy and liturgical propriety over heartfelt practical piety. From Frelinghuysen, he absorbed a uniquely pietistic perspective on the process of salvation, the importance of conversion and the methods by which conversion and piety might best be promoted.[4]

Although their ethnic and ecclesiastical pedigrees were quite different, the ministries of the Presbyterian William Tennent and the Dutch Reformed Frelinghuysen exhibited several striking similarities. Both men attacked hypocritical participation in the sacraments. Both opposed the idea that one's childhood training, ethnic origin, or theological acumen assured salvation. Both stressed the internal intention of the individual over the external observance of ethical or liturgical rules, and both emphasized the need for repentance, conversion, and a sincere practice of piety.

These shared beliefs facilitated Gilbert Tennent's acceptance of Frelinghuysen as his second mentor when he assumed responsibility for his first church in New Brunswick, New Jersey, where Frelinghuysen served a Dutch Reformed congregation. In Frelinghuysen's ministry Gilbert discovered a theology and practice basically in sympathy with the teachings of his father and yet more powerful than the elder Tennent's pastorate because Frelinghuysen focused upon conversion as the central experience of the Christian life. William Tennent, Sr., preached the need for conversion in the Christian disciple, but compared to Frelinghuysen, he gave it a secondary place in his preaching. As Martin E. Lodge has noted,

> A Tennent sermon of 1729 speaks of this experience [of conversion] as the "first act of illumination." . . . It marks the infusion of the grace of God into the sinner, and is but the first step in a growth in obedience, humility, and the understanding of God's teaching. Though such conversion is "deeply affecting" and "humbling to the soul," it is not the shattering experience of Frelinghuysen's evangelism.

According to Lodge, then, the elder Tennent emphasized the Christian's " 'growth in grace' rather than the actual experience of conversion."[5]

Gilbert Tennent never entirely abandoned his father's concern for the Christian's growth in grace, but he increasingly envisioned this spiritual progress in terms of a three-step paradigm for conversion that he learned from the German-born Pietist, Frelinghuysen. Frelinghuysen's ministry had been dramatically shaped by contacts early in his career with two groups of Dutch Reformed Pietists in East Friesland. From these colleagues he learned that salvation required the successful negotiation of three stages. The first was conviction; the second, conversion; and the third, a life of sincere practical piety. Conviction resulted from the pointed presentation of the Old Testament's stringent ethical demands. This convinced sinners that they were incapable of achieving a morally pure life-style when left to their own devices and, hence, were subject to God's terrible wrath and damnation. Conviction also prepared the sinful heart for the gospel by priming the pained sinner to accept Christ's "good news," which itself offered the soothing promise of forgiveness and the much-needed opportunity to begin life anew through an experience of gracious rebirth. New birth or conversion naturally followed and was the most important landmark on the salvation road. But it had to culminate in a life of exemplary Christian piety, since such a witness was the inevitable fruit of grace in the human heart.[6] Because Tennent came to accept this model for the Christian life, and particularly its stress on new birth as the key step in the journey to salvation, his sermons began to correspond more closely in style and content to those of his Dutch colleague. This modification in Tennent's ministry had two important long-term effects on Awakening history. First, it transformed an otherwise ineffectual New Jersey pastor into a major revival figure in the middle colonies, and, second, it laid the foundation for Tennent's future relations with the Puritan-educated Presbyterian pastors of northern New Jersey and New York.

Tennent's career blossomed during his apprenticeship under Frelinghuysen. In the late 1720s Tennent sparked his first major revivals among colonial Presbyterians. In 1735 he produced his earliest published work, *A Solemn Warning to the Secure World*, which was one of the sermons responsible for his success. This publication is critical for understanding Tennent's Awakening ministry for two reasons. First, it illustrates his debt to Frelinghuysen's Pietism, and, second, it contains his own theological explanation of revival homiletics.[7]

Like his father and Frelinghuysen before him, Tennent believed that humanity's pretenses to righteousness were far greater obstacles to human salvation than willful vice. The arrogant affectation of spiritual propriety obstructed the sinner's view of his or her vices, and made the sinful person comfortable and secure in the quagmire of unrighteousness. The clergy were responsible for awakening sinners from this deadly security, but to do so they had to preach terrors. Preaching the terrors involved the annihilation of self-righteousness, first by exposing its sources, and second by comparing the sinner's supposed good works with the humanly impossible perfection demanded in the biblical law.

Although the sources of self-righteousness were legion, Tennent singled out thirteen common causes of the deadly malady. Each of these factors kept the sinner ignorant of his or her sin by discouraging careful self-examination and by leading the unrighteous to judge their spiritual condition by surface appearances. Thus, the sinful were persuaded that a pious education, a good social reputation, formal church membership, or orthodox beliefs were sufficient evidences of a right relationship with God. But Tennent warned that "all presumptuous Persons are not guilty of Prophaneness or Immorality, no, no; some of them make a fair shew in the Flesh, are regular in their external Conduct, and have the strict *Form* of Godliness, though they are destitute of the Power of it." Therefore, self-satisfaction rather than overt impropriety was the truest mark of the sinner.[8]

The major external agent perpetuating the sinner's deadly self-righteousness was the Devil, of course, but his most capable human ally was the unconverted clergyman. In Tennent's view, ministers who had not experienced a second birth through grace were a dangerous fifth column in the church. They maintained a "loose Carriage" and a "frothy, chatty, jocose Discourse" in their social relations. They neglected their duty to examine sinners' souls by allowing a "lax and promiscuous admission of unworthy Guests" at the communion table and by discussing "the erroneous, nature soothing, but soul damning Doctrines of Free Will, universal Grace, and universal Redemption" in their preaching. Seeking personal honor and gain rather than the salvation of sinners, these men catered to graceless people's wish "to hear of nothing but Love, Peace, Promises [and] Comforts." They avoided offense by classifying "their Audience into one common mass" so that no one recognized his or her own graceless state, and they applied the terrors of the biblical law and the comforts of the gospel out of sequence so that conviction seemed unnecessary for conversion.[9]

Tennent addressed two barbed questions to the smooth and soothing practice of his unconverted associates. "Are not Ministers called the Salt of the Earth? [And] has not Salt a biting, painful Quality?" The answer was obvious. The ministry was both biting and painful to sinners because the clergy were ordained to awaken fallen humanity from its deep sleep of false security. The manifold causes of human self-deception made this task difficult and necessitated a far more violent method than that practiced by "once-born" ministers of his day.[10]

Tennent compared the preacher to an individual whose neighbor was "sleeping securely and dreaming pleasantly" while his house was afire. In such a situation, Tennent observed,

> You would not surely go to whisper in . . . [your neighbor's] Ear some soft round about Discourse, that his House was you feared

> not in the best Condition possible, [and that] it might perhaps take Damage if suitable Care were not taken to prevent it. I say would you go thus about the Bush with a poor Man in a Time of such Danger? No, I believe not: I fancy you would take a rougher method, without Ceremony or Grimace.

By the same logic, Tennent declared that preaching terrors was the proper method of a saving ministry. Although it was jarring, preaching terrors was more merciful than the soft homiletics of unconverted ministers since it alone saved sinners from the horrible pain of eternal damnation.[11]

The comforting promises of the gospel so commonly found in the preaching of the unconverted had their place in Tennent's sermons, but they were not so indiscriminately applied. Tennent reserved Christianity's good news for those sinners already convicted of their sins, and he preceded all such soothing discourse with the threat of terrors for those not yet convinced of their evil nature. In his *Solemn Warning*, Tennent justified this homiletic pattern in three ways. First, he claimed that the sequence of "terrors first, comforts second" coincided with God's own treatment of the soul. The Holy Spirit converted the human heart by convicting it of its sins before supplying the gospel balsam to sin's deep wound. It was appropriate, then, that the clergy should synchronize their public proclamations to the Spirit's internal actions. The presentation of terrors before comforts was justified by "natural reason" as well. Tennent noted that wise builders did not build their houses before digging deep foundations, nor did experienced farmers sow their fields before plowing the sun-hardened soil. So too, Tennent claimed, good ministers should not build faith before digging a deep foundation of conviction in the soul, or sow gospel seeds before applying the plow of terrors to sin-hardened hearts. As a final rationale for his preaching style, Tennent pointed to the psychological handicaps of fallen humanity.

> Unconverted People have a clearer Notion of Pain, both bodily and mental, than of the Pleasures and Comforts of a pious life, for They have had the Experience of the one, but not of the other . . . Unconverted people are [also] governed . . . by Hatred against the good God; . . . How then can it be reasonably expected that such Persons will be much moved by Love Arguments when they are without that noble generous *Passion* in any Degree of *Luminence* towards God.

According to Tennent, sinners could not be expected to respond to that which they did not understand or apprehend. Therefore, they must be awakened in the only way their crippled natures would allow, that is, through the threatened pain of terrible damnation.[12]

The pietistic approach to spiritual revival summarized in Tennent's

Solemn Warning was vehemently opposed by a group of middle-colony Presbyterian clergymen known to historians as the subscriptionists. These men hoped to revitalize their denomination by using the Philadelphia Synod to impose stricter regulations on their fellow ministers' educational qualifications, theology and practice. They found Tennent's approach objectionable for two reasons. First, they assumed the New Brunswick pastor's harsh words for unconverted ministers would diminish the laity's respect for the clergy generally, and second, they suspected that Tennent was willing to abandon presbyterian order and Calvinist theology in the name of promoting new birth.[13]

The subscriptionists used their numerical superiority during the late 1730s to pass two acts aimed at controlling the spread of revival fever. The first restricted the movements of Presbyterian revivalists outside their local presbyteries; the second tightened Synod oversight of ministerial candidates who had not attended a chartered colonial college but instead had received their theological education from the pro-revival William Tennent, Sr.[14]

These measures might have accomplished their purpose of throttling the Awakening had Presbyterian revivalists remained an isolated party in their church. But this was not to be. Between 1738 and 1745 Tennent courted the favor of a third contingent of ministers within the Synod's membership. Led by Jonathan Dickinson of Elizabethtown, this group of clergymen served Presbyterians in northern New Jersey and New York. The majority of these men had been educated in New England, and, consequently, they had great respect for the congregational polity and experiential theology of American Puritanism.

Their theological tradition's *pater familias*, English Puritanism, had played a seminal role in the formation of seventeenth-century Dutch Reformed Pietism, so Dickinson's Puritan party shared certain convictions with Gilbert Tennent.[15] Indeed, those views held in common by William Tennent, Sr., and Theodorus Frelinghuysen were integral parts of the Puritan perspective. On these points of agreement Tennent forged an alliance with the Presbyterians north of New Brunswick and thereby overpowered the obstructionist policies of subscriptionists in his church.

Because Puritan Presbyterians initially harbored serious doubts about certain aspects of Tennent's pietistic revival approach, this alliance was not easily formed. Dickinson and his associates found Gilbert's stress on new birth entirely acceptable. From the time of first settlement, New England churches had demanded that their members, and especially their clergy, possess a firsthand knowledge of God's gracious work in the human heart. But where the first generation of New England Puritans had believed that an individual should not be accepted into full membership before his or her experience of new birth had been judged valid,

Dickinson tended to balance his interest in Christian conversion with a strong insistence on doctrinal orthodoxy, respect for the ordained clergy, and the recognition that ultimately God alone knew the true state of a human soul.[16]

In a sermon of 1739 Dickinson acknowledged his doubts about humanity's ability to judge the spiritual condition of lay or clerical associates. Dickinson was sure that the most humble and serious Christian would not boast about his or her attainments in grace. Therefore, he proposed that those who spoke the least about their conversion were most likely better acquainted with it than their more loquacious neighbors. Dickinson also noted that the pattern of spiritual rebirth was far more variable than revival supporters supposed. As he put it, the "holy one of Israel" cannot be limited to any one method of conversion. So, one has no certain standard by which to measure the new birth of a fellow Christian.[17]

The views of Gilbert Tennent and his mentor, Frelinghuysen, more closely resembled the theology of early New England Puritans than the theology of their contemporary Puritan neighbors. But the similarity was generated by the familiarity of the two men with continental Pietism rather than by any personal knowledge of early Puritan practices.

The Dutch Reformed Pietists who had taught Frelinghuysen how to preach the Christian gospel believed that the clergyman's duty to inspire rebirth in his parishioners presupposed a prior judgment of their spiritual condition. These Pietist pastors recognized that God was free to save sinners in any fashion he chose. Therefore, there was no perfect yardstick by which spiritual development could be gauged. Yet they believed that educated guesses were possible and, indeed, required. They were possible because the divine creator was not an arbitrary sovereign. His Spirit's operations on the human heart followed a predictable course in the norm, and this pattern could serve as a guide for determining whether an individual's experience exhibited the typical signs of spiritual renewal. Furthermore, evaluations of spiritual progress were required so that the clergy could preach terrors to the secure and the gospel to the convicted in the appropriate season.

This belief in the necessity of judging others, Frelinghuysen acquired in the Netherlands and passed along to Gilbert Tennent. But Dickinson and his associates would not accept its logic. Indeed, Dickinson maintained that the judgmental practice of the revival ministers and laity was like "a dead Fly in the Apothecaries Ointment" that seriously undermined the Awakening's potential healing powers.[18]

So long as this remained the opinion of the New York clergy, Gilbert Tennent had no chance of overcoming Presbyterian subscriptionist opposition. Fortunately for the New Brunswick pastor, however, events conspired to favor his cause. During the same month in which Dickinson exposed his objections to Pietist revivalism, George Whitefield arrived in Lewistown, Delaware. Whitefield planned to tour the middle colonies, but his first project was a journey to New York City. This offered Tennent the opportunity to use the dynamic English evangelist to quiet his Puritan colleagues' apprehensions.[19]

Whitefield began his travels on November 12 after resting a few days in Philadelphia. His second stop was Gilbert Tennent's parish in New Brunswick. Tennent was ten years Whitefield's senior, but the two men quickly discovered that their theological and pastoral interests were almost identical: Like Tennent, Whitefield preached the necessity of a new birth in Christ and cooperated willingly with the clergy and laity of other communions who emphasized the same message. In later years, Whitefield would find Tennent's ecumenism more limited than his own since the Presbyterian balked at intimate association with non-Calvinists. But during this first meeting, differences in the approaches of the two men were not yet evident. Therefore, Whitefield accepted Tennent's offer to accompany him on his trip to New York City.[20]

The potential benefit to Tennent of the Whitefield tour became obvious to the New Brunswick pastor as soon as he learned that the English evangelist planned to travel through northern New Jersey and New York City. As Whitefield's guide, Tennent could steer his new friend to those churches where Puritan Presbyterian leaders served and, with a little prior briefing, perhaps even determine the message that Whitefield preached from these pulpits.

It is impossible to know exactly how much Tennent manipulated Whitefield's itinerary, but it is clear that his ultimate objective was achieved. Whitefield's phenomenal success during his first tour in the middle colonies forced the Dickinson party to consider again the possibility that the previous Tennent revivals had been a foretaste of a truly monumental work of God in America. Moreover, Whitefield's frequent attacks on ministers who were "well versed in the doctrines of grace, having learned them at university, but notwithstanding are heart hypocrites, and enemies to the power of godliness" laid seeds of doubt about the motives of subscriptionist opposition to the revivals. As these seeds took root and later trips by Whitefield generated unmistakable evidence of a general colonial awakening of spiritual concern, Dickinson and his colleagues moved closer and closer to an alliance with Tennent.[21]

By 1741 only one barrier stood in the way of total cooperation between Puritan and Pietist Presbyterians in the New Jersey–New York area. That was Tennent's continued policy of judging the state of others' souls. This obstacle was surmounted, however, when Tennent learned the potential dangers of his approach rather inadvertently from the wild antics of a revival colleague and the rivalry of Moravian Awakening sympathizers.

In July 1741 Connecticut and Rhode Island were invaded by James Davenport, a Presbyterian revivalist from Southhold, Long Island. Davenport had cooperated with Tennent in a famous Society Hill revival in Philadelphia during 1740 and had served as a pulpit supply in Tennent's congregation during one of Gilbert's frequent absences. But Davenport's tour through southern New England scandalized Tennent and brought opprobrium on the entire Awakening movement.[22]

Davenport carried the practice of judging souls beyond anything Tennent had yet imagined. Wherever he traveled, Davenport asked local pastors to give him an account of their personal conversion. If they refused, Davenport judged them unregenerate sinners and declared as much in his next public sermon. Tennent had never openly made such demands of ordained clergymen, and he did not expose the names of his unconverted colleagues from the pulpit. To his way of thinking, such charges were best reserved for formal ecclesiastical courts.[23]

Yet many of Tennent's contemporaries saw little difference between Tennent's policy and that of Davenport. Others viewed Davenport as more honest than Tennent, or at least more merciful, since he specified which men he opposed while Tennent's indiscriminate attacks on the unconverted ministry stained the reputation and undermined the authority of all clergymen. Tennent was convinced that Davenport's practice was quite different from his own, but the episode planted doubts in his mind that were later nurtured to full growth by the actions of Moravian Awakening sympathizers.

The *Unitas Fratrum* (or Moravian church) originated during the Bohemian Hussite rebellion of pre-Reformation Europe, but it was reshaped in the eighteenth century by the fertile mind of its major patron and leader, the German Pietist Count Nicholas Zinzendorf. Zinzendorf reformed the Moravian fellowship into an umbrella church by introducing his own peculiar brand of Pietism into the communion's theology. The new *Unitas Fratrum* welcomed members from all Christian organizations. In the Moravian church, the rites and dogmas of the members' former denominations were respected but not emphasized in the interest of Christian unity. Like Pietists elsewhere in Europe and America, Moravians assumed that the essential badge of Christian discipleship was spiritual rebirth rather than doctrinal orthodoxy or ritual propriety. In contrast to Dutch Reformed and German Lutheran Pietists, though, the Moravians insisted that twice-born Christians should manifest their common experience and commitment in concrete form by associating in a single ecclesiastical body.[24]

Despite the fact that the Moravians supported the central thrust of the Awakening, Tennent vehemently opposed their program. Tennent was a Pietist, but he was also a Reformed clergyman. He believed the Moravians' untempered ecumenism was potentially dangerous since it encouraged the laity to ignore their theological base.[25]

Tennent's attack on the Moravians split the revival movement. As one contemporary observer noted, Moravian sympathizers began to treat Tennent "in the same uncharitable, censorious, imperious, divisive Manner" that the Presbyterian revivalist had previously treated "the Body of the Clergy." Put another way, Moravian sympathizers began to ask whether Tennent was himself converted, just as Tennent had formerly questioned the experiential qualification of his Presbyterian opponents.[26]

With the finger of judgment pointed in his direction for a change, Tennent responded by moderating his support of spiritual estimates of the state of his clerical and lay associates' souls. In 1744 a chastened Tennent confessed that "the longer Gracious Persons live, and the more they know of the Deceits of their own Hearts, the more sensible they will be of their unfitness to judge of the States of others, and the less inclin'd they will be to it."[27]

This new humility in Tennent opened the way for a final alliance between revivalists of his persuasion and the Puritan Presbyterians of northern New Jersey and New York. As early as 1742 Dickinson noted that Tennent had acquired a "cool and Catholic Spirit." By 1745 Tennent's proclamations against rash judgments were sufficiently frequent and convincing to lead Dickinson and his colleagues to join with him in the formation of a new synod. This New York Synod became the organizational base for Presbyterian Awakening activity for the remaining years of the movement, and its establishment insured the ultimate victory of revival interests in the Presbyterian church.[28]

Tennent's triumph was, however, a pyrrhic victory both for the Great Awakening in his home region and for his future reputation in American history. Tennent's conflict with the Moravians inadvertently united the Presbyterian communion, but it also significantly contributed to the destruction in the middle colonies of the interdenominational cooperation upon which the Awakening movement depended. Increasingly Awakeners recognized the destructive effects of the revivals on their followers' denominational and theological allegiances. Like Tennent, they feared the attraction of the Moravians' ecumenical posture, for which their own promotion of the Awakening had laid the groundwork. Thus, they followed Tennent in reemphasizing their denominational ties.

For Awakening historiography, Tennent's forced modifications of his pietistic views had an equally dramatic long-term consequence—his eclipse by his Puritan contemporaries in the retelling of American history. Because American religious historians have been only moderately familiar with Tennent's early theological development, they have assumed that his revival ministry was no more than a minor (though boisterous) variation on the Puritan Awakener motif. Thus, Tennent has received frequent honorable mention but no concentrated attention.

Tennent in fact, though, represented a theological strand in the Awakening that differed significantly from that of Edwards, Dickinson or any of the other Puritan revivalists. His pietistic orientation hailed from the European Continent rather than New or Old England and, in the middle colonies, was more responsible for sparking revival fever than the influence of Edwards and as important in sustaining Awakening fervor as the preaching of Whitefield.

Notes

1. Examples of this approach are too numerous to mention in full, but a few of the most important recent works are the following: Richard L. Bushman, *From Puritan to Yankee: Character and the Social Order in Connecticut, 1690–1765* (Cambridge, Mass.: Harvard University Press, 1967); Edwin Scott Gaustad, *The Great Awakening in New England* (New York: Harper and Row, 1957); C. C. Goen, *Revivalism and Separatism in New England: Strict Congregationalists and Separate Baptists in the Great Awakening* (New Haven: Yale University Press, 1962); Alan Heimert and Perry Miller, eds., "Introduction," in *The Great Awakening: Documents Illustrating the Crisis and Its Consequences* (Indianapolis, Ind.: Bobbs-Merrill Co., 1967) pp. xiii–lxi; Alan Heimert, *Religion and the American Mind: From the Great Awakening to the Revolution* (Cambridge, Mass.: Harvard University Press, 1966).

2. New research on Dutch Reformed Pietism is based on two older works that represented the major scholarship on the subject up until quite recently. Those volumes are Heinrich Heppe, *Geschichte des Pietismus und der Mystik in der Reformierten Kirche* (Leiden: E. J. Brill, 1879) and Wilhelm Goeters, *Die Vorbereiting des Pietismus in der Reformierten Kirche der Niederlande* (Leipzig: J. C. Hinrichs, 1911). More current examinations of the subject include J. van den Berg and J. P. Van Dooren, eds., *Pietismus und Reveil* (Leiden: E. J. Brill, 1978); George Brown, Jr., "Pietism and the Reformed Tradition," *Reformed Review* 23(1970):143–52; M. Eugene Ostenhaven, "The Experimental Theology of Early Dutch Calvinism," *Reformed Review* 27 (Spring, 1974): 180–89; Martin H. Prozesky, "The Emergence of Dutch Pietism," *Journal of Ecclesiastical History* 28 (January 1977): 29–37; F. Ernest Stoeffler, ed., *Continental Pietism and Early American Christianity* (Grand Rapids, Mich.: William B. Eerdmans Publishing Co., 1976); F. Ernest Stoeffler, *The Rise of Evangelical Pietism*, Studies in the History of Religions, Vol. 9 (Leiden: E. J. Brill, 1965); James Tanis, *Dutch Calvinistic Pietism in the Middle Colonies: A Study in the Life and Theology of Theodorus Jacobus Frelinghuysen* (The Hague: Martinus Nijhoff, 1967).

3. No biography of Gilbert Tennent has been published and only two dissertations have focused on Gilbert Tennent's career. They are Miles Douglas Harper, "Gilbert Tennent, Theologian of the 'New Light' " (Ph.D. diss., Duke University, 1958) and Milton J Coalter, Jr., "The Life of Gilbert Tennent: A Case Study of Continental Pietism's Influence on the First Great Awakening in the Middle Colonies" (Ph.D. diss., Princeton University, 1982).

4. For the best biographical treatments of William Tennent, Sr., see Thomas C. Pears,

Jr., *Documentary History of William Tennent and the Log College* (Philadelphia: Department of History, General Assembly of the Presbyterian Church in the United States of America, 1940); Archibald Alexander, *Biographical Sketches of the Founder and Principal Alumni of the Log College* (Philadelphia: Presbyterian Board of Publications, 1851); George H. Ingram, "Biographies of the Alumni of the Log College: II William Tennent, Sr., The Founder," *Journal of Presbyterian History* 14 (March 1930): 1–27; and Mary A. Tennent, *Light in Darkness: The Story of William Tennent, Sr. and the Log College* (Greensboro, N.C.: Greensboro Printing Co., 1971). The best study of Frelinghuysen's career is Tanis, *Dutch Calvinistic Pietism.*

5. Martin E. Lodge, "The Great Awakening in the Middle Colonies" (Ph.D. diss., University of California, Berkeley, 1964), p. 128.

6. Tanis, *Dutch Calvinistic Pietism*, pp. 36–37, 114–132.

7. Gilbert Tennent, *A Solemn Warning to the Secure World, from the God of Terrible Majesty Or, The Presumptuous Sinner Detected, his Pleas Consider'd, and his Doom Display'd* (Boston: S. Kneeland and T. Green, 1735).

8. Ibid., 2, 12, 15–32, 34, 50, 85, 87–88, 97, 102.

9. Ibid., 97–102.

10. Ibid., 99.

11. Ibid., 72–73.

12. Ibid., 70–71.

13. *An Examination and Refutation of Mr. Gilbert Tennent's Remarks Upon the Protestation Presented to the Synod of Philadelphia, June 1, 1741; And the said Protest set in its True Light, and Justified. By Some Members of the Synod* (Philadelphia: Benjamin Franklin 1742); [Robert Cross], *A Protestation Presented to the Synod of Philadelphia: June 1, 1741* (Philadelphia: Benjamin Franklin, 1741).

14. Guy S. Klett, ed., *Minutes of Presbyterian Church in America, 1706–1788*, (Philadelphia: Presbyterian Historical Society, 1976), pp. 153–54, 157.

15. Stoeffler, *Rise of Evangelical Pietism*, pp. 116–121.

16. David D. Hall, *The Faithful Shepherd: A History of the New England Ministry in the Seventeenth Century* (Chapel Hill: University of North Carolina Press, for the Institute of Early American History & Culture, 1972), pp. 54–55.

17. Jonathan Dickinson, *The Danger of Schisms and Contentions with Respect to the Ministry and Ordinances of the Gospel, presented in a Sermon Preached at the Meeting of the Presbytery at Woodbridge, October 10th, 1739* (New York: J. Peter Zenger, 1739), pp. 20–21.

18. Ibid., 22.

19. *George Whitefield's Journals*, intro., William V. Davis (1905; facsimile edition, Gainesville, Florida: Scholar's Facsimiles and Reprints, 1969), pp. 334–36.

20. Ibid., 342–44.

21. Ibid., 134.

22. The best narrative accounts of Davenport's activities in New England can be found in Richard Webster, *A History of the Presbyterian Church in America, from its Origin until the Year 1760* (Philadelphia: Joseph M. Wilson, 1857), pp. 537–41; and Goen, *Revivalism and Separatism*, pp. 20–25.

23. Webster, *History of the Presbyterian Church* pp. 537–41; Goen, *Revivalism*, pp. 20–25; Gilbert Tennent to Jonathan Dickinson, 12 February 1742 in *Boston Weekly News Letter,* 15–22 July 1742.

24. Excellent treatments of Zinzendorf's ecumenical pietist views can be found in Theodor Wettach, *Kirche bei Zinzendorf* (Wuppertal: Rolf Brockhaus, 1971), pp. 59–71; F. Ernest Stoeffler, *German Pietism During the Eighteenth Century*, Studies in the History of Religions, vol. 24 (Leiden: E. J. Brill, 1973), pp. 156–59; and Arthur J. Lewis, *Zinzendorf, the Ecumenical Pioneer: A Study in the Moravian Contribution to Christian Mission and Unity* (Philadelphia: Westminster Press, 1962), pp. 138–60.

25. Milton J Coalter, Jr., "The Radical Pietism of Count Nicholas Zinzendorf as a Conservative Influence on the Awakener, Gilbert Tennent," *Church History* 49 (March 1980): 35–46.

26. [John Hancock], *The Examiner, Or Gilbert against Tennent* . . . (1743; reprint Philadelphia: B. Franklin, 1743), p. 31.

27. Gilbert Tennent, *The Necessity of Studying to be Quiet, and Doing Our Own Business* (Philadelphia: William Bradford, [1744]), pp. 10–11.

28. Jonathan Dickinson to Colonel Alford, 12 April 1742, Thomas Foxcroft Correspondence, Firestone Library, Princeton University, Princeton, New Jersey.

The Mechanics of Revival: New Jersey Presbyterians During the Second Awakening

Martha T. Blauvelt

Martha T. Blauvelt is an associate professor of history at the College of Saint Benedict in St. Joseph, Minnesota. She is the author of essays on women and revivalism in volumes 1 and 2 of *Women and Religion in America: A Documentary History*.

IN 1832, AT THE HEIGHT OF THE Second Awakening, Calvin Colton concluded that "revivals of religion have been gradually multiplying, until they have become the grand absorbing theme and aim of the American religious world."[1] Historians have since affirmed the importance of revivalism in American life and have investigated the origins of religious concern in great detail. But not since the great revival manuals of the nineteenth century has the form of the revival—as opposed to its sociopsychological origins—received the attention it deserves.[2] We know little about the roles played by clergy and laity or the steps or the structure of the small-town revivals common to the settled parts of America before the rise of Charles Grandison Finney's New Measures. In neglecting the mechanics of these revivals, we miss an opportunity of understanding how the revival reflected and transformed local church life and values, and how it influenced the character of popular evangelism. An investigation of the revival form among New Jersey Presbyterians suggests how changes in revival structure affected the quality of religious enthusiasm, lay behavior, and clerical authority during the Second Awakening.

The Second Awakening's revival form evolved between 1739 and 1800; by the beginning of the nineteenth century, it was fully developed. Its revival structure was the product of the growing commitment of New Jersey Presbyterianism to evangelicalism and its continuous search for an effective evangelical technique. That commitment and its expression in the religious revival originated in the First Awakening. Only by looking at revivals in the First Awakening and the decades succeeding it can we understand the origins of the Second Awakening's revival form.

Revivals among New Jersey Presbyterians during the First Awakening had little in common with early nineteenth-century revivals. Those earlier revivals centered on charismatic itinerant preachers: men of great personal force and an apparent ability to see into the human heart who were bent on a personal mission to save sinners.[3] In New Jersey not only George Whitefield but also Joseph Morgan, Samuel Blair, Gilbert and William Tennent, Samuel Finley and other Presbyterian ministers played this role.[4] For the colony's laity, who were by and large unfamiliar with revivals, the appearance of a committed, magnetic evangelist had the character of a divine visitation.

It was just this dependence on the charismatic preacher which encouraged the Awakening's disorder and emotionalism. The true extent of the Awakening's turbulence is difficult to determine: the Old Side exaggerated it, and New Side ministers (who wrote the revival accounts of this period) minimized it. Even then, they described "great Horror and Trembling, and loud Weeping"; people "overcome and fainting; others deeply sobbing, hardly able to contain [themselves]" or showing "strange unusual bodily Motions." Whitefield's *Journals* also show that men and women often fell to the ground, groaning and begging for mercy, upon hearing the Awakener's compelling message.[5] The personal magnetism and "searching" sermons of Whitefield and other evangelists, combined with the laity's unfamiliarity with mass revival meetings, encouraged an emotional religiosity which culminated in the excesses of James Davenport and his followers.

In contrast to later Presbyterian revivals, the laity had no independent role in creating religious enthusiasm during the First Awakening. The near unanimity with which New Jersey's Presbyterian clergy embraced evangelicalism made such lay activities as public preaching or separation unnecessary.[6] Presbyterian lay persons confined themselves to choosing between Old and New Side ministers—an important power, but one which still left them dependent on the preacher to initiate a revival. Unfamiliar with revivals and, in many cases, with evangelical theology, the laity lacked the authority and initiative in spiritual matters that it had long since attained in the church's financial affairs. Independent lay efforts to foster revivals were therefore rare, although men and women might counsel each other once a revival was in progress. Only in Maidenhead and Hopewell were there a number of lay persons "truly acquainted with vital Religion" and "earnest in Prayer Night and Day to have the Gospel in Power among them." Their pastor recognized that lay prayers had helped start their 1739–40 revival, and that they had aided its progress by "conversing with the Convinced" until they were "come thro' to sound Conversion."[7]

The Presbyterian revivals of the First Awakening centered on the charismatic preacher, but they ultimately inspired a great deal of lay activity and organization. Evangelical zeal was one characteristic of the Awakening's converts: as William Tennent noted, they "rejoice in *Zion's* Prosperity; glorifying GOD on that Account, and feel a Sympathy in her Sorrows."[8] This fervor seems to have been a natural result of the conversion process. Jacob Green of Massachusetts, for example, who had been converted under Gilbert Tennent's preaching and who would become Hanover's Presbyterian pastor, experienced "a strong, longing desire for the good of souls, and wished and prayed fervently for the conversion and salvation of others."[9]

In the years after the Awakening, New Side clergy welcomed such zeal in the laity. Ministers did so partly in an effort to share their own evangelical responsibilities. In the 1740s and 50s, as New Side principles rose to prominence in the church, Presbyterians redefined the ministry: the conversion of sinners succeeded the inculcation of morals as the clergyman's chief function. All pastors were to seek the revivals which charismatic itinerants had fostered during the Awakening. It was their duty to "alarm a secure World, by opening the Meaning, and denouncing the Threats of the Law against the Impenitent, that so they may be storm'd out of their false Refuges, and compell'd to fly to Jesus for Protection."[10] Ordination sermons reminded ministers that they might "either be the Instrument of saving our Hearers or of aggravating their future Condemnation."[11]

This was a responsibility many ministers found heavy. Pastors such as Caleb Smith of Newark Mountains were "much affected" by the thought that their ministry "would be either a Savour of Life unto Life, or of Death unto Death to others; and that Ministers must give an Account of the Souls committed to their Care."[12] In accordance with eighteenth-century Presbyterian theology, the clergy believed that the Holy Spirit alone could cause revivals, yet the popular understanding of the ministry made their worth dependent on their ability to convert sinners. Caught in this dilemma, ministers increasingly turned to the laity to share evangelical responsibilities. In their eagerness to fulfill the goals of their Church and office, ministers found lay activity more an aid than a threat.[13] And indeed, the efforts of pious parishioners, coming as they did from within the community, were far easier to control than were intruding itinerants. At the same time, devout lay persons possessed both the willingness and the experience to play effective roles in revivals.

The Awakening provided not only lay zeal but organizations with which to express that zeal. The Awakening's preachers noted that converts set aside "youthful extravagancies" for "religious Conversation"; they established prayer societies even before revivals ended.[14] These groups assured that new converts' enthusiasm for "*Zion's* Prosperity" would not fade away, but would develop into a sense of responsibility for their church's spiritual well-being. Continued association with revival members also prolonged the convert's memory of his first mass religious experience and encouraged him to judge his community by that high standard. At the same time, lay societies helped preserve the historical memory of revivals and the way they worked. They thus both heightened sensitivity to declension and provided the knowledge and organizational impetus needed to combat it.

The First Awakening also furnished what, as Calvin Colton later observed, was "most of all indispensable" for the development of evangelicalism: "a faith in the doctrine—in the possibility, the importance, and the reality" of revivals.[15] Before the Awakening, most New Jersey

Presbyterians had lacked this faith: they scarcely knew what a revival was. But the simple fact that so many Presbyterians underwent the revival experience between 1739 and 1743 familiarized them with mass religious emotion, impressed them with the possibility of national reformation, and created in them a desire for further revivals. At the same time, this experience made it likely that later revivals would be substantially different from those of the First Awakening. It provided first that a devout laity, now familiar with revivals, concerned for "*Zion's* Prosperity," and organized in prayer societies, would take a more important role. Secondly, it made emotionalism much less likely: not only were ministers more aware of how to handle the convicted, but after James Davenport's excesses they were determined not to let emotion mar future revivals and imperil the reputation of evangelical religion. In addition, the existence of devout Christians who had themselves undergone the stages of conversion provided a source of stability and guidance. After the First Awakening, the Presbyterian revival progressively lost its emotional, charismatic character and became an organized communal rite.

Elizabethtown's second revival, in 1771–72, illustrates the rapidity with which this transition occurred in some towns.[16] The origins of this revival lay in 1768, when a member of the congregation developed an "uneasiness" about "the amazing [spiritual] stupidity and slothfulness of christians in general." By 1769 he had established a prayer society composed of four young men which met every Saturday evening for prayers; it also informally attempted to "awaken" sinners. At this point the minister, James Caldwell, who had been away for six months, returned and, at the behest of this society, established catechizing lectures. At first only ten to twelve people attended these lectures, yet they helped to both arouse sinners and stir "up to greater diligence those who had religion, but had been asleep ever since the last revival here." Caldwell officially recognized the role of the prayer society members by meeting with them every Monday night "to consult measures for the reviving of religion among us." Each member chose a particular person to whom he was "most likely to be useful," and strove with that person either until conversion was effected or there was no encouragement to proceed further. In addition, Caldwell sometimes told the society the subjects he intended to preach on; this enabled it to correlate its efforts with the next sermon. In contrast to the First Awakening, where the clergyman had the sole initiative, the laity and their minister worked hand in hand to create conditions conducive to a revival.[17] In this case, the devout began their efforts even before their pastor, although their subsequent activities remained under his direction.

The 1771–72 revival was as controlled and organized in process as it was in inception. The Saturday evening prayer society expanded to admit the newly converted, who numbered as high as 150. Again working together, Caldwell gave "pathetical and pointed" lectures, while the original members of the society presided over the meetings. In the meantime, the Monday evening methods group evolved into a public meeting which discussed difficult Biblical texts and cases of conscience, and those already converted created another society which studied the Scriptures and set aside fifteen minutes every Monday, Wednesday, and Friday morning to pray for the "influence of the Holy Spirit." In this controlled environment, emotion, with the exception of restrained weeping, did not break out. Rather than culminating in religious passion, as had the First Awakening, Elizabeth Town's 1771–72 revival resulted in a church membership gain of 110 and the establishment of twenty-one prayer groups.

Elizabethtown's 1771–72 revival illustrates the beginning of the shift between what Calvin Colton saw as two distinct revival types: "one, when the instruments are not apparent; the other, when the instruments are obvious." Because the First Awakening's revivals had been structured around a charismatic preacher, they had seemed to occur arbitrarily, according to God's will. From the congregation's perspective, "nobody expected, nobody prayed, nobody tried for such a work—so far as appeared."[18] But as local clergy and laity began to work actively and publicly for a revival, it began to lose its mystery. Between 1745 and 1800 the revival was progressively demystified as New Jersey Presbyterians experienced local revivals such as Elizabethtown's.[19] These revivals also provided a new pool of dedicated Christians who replaced the First Awakening's converts. When John McDowell became pastor of the Elizabethtown Presbyterian Church in 1804, for example, he found that nearly all his elders and almost half his church members were "fruits" of a 1784–85 revival.[20] By 1800 countless New Jersey Presbyterians had participated in a new revival form—one which would find its fullest expression in the revivals of the Second Awakening.

Why Americans in the early nineteenth century were so responsive to revival techniques remains obscure, but what those techniques were is clear. The Second Awakening was the product of organization, not a charismatic individual. A major force in organizing this religious revival was the laity. It is clear from the innumerable accounts of Second Awakening revivals that lay persons had fully accepted the evangelical responsibilities ministers had pressed upon them during the eighteenth century. By then church members regarded it as their fault if religion declined in their community. Sensitized to declension by revival memories and evangelical expectations, the devout believed "something must be done" about any perceived decline in piety. They organized prayer meetings in which they bewailed their own failings and the sins of the community and asked God to visit them with a divine work.[21]

Their fervor is evident in Reverend Asa Hillyer's description of an 1807 prayer society in the Orange Presbyterian Church, a society which had been meeting since the 1760s: "Such fervent and earnest wrestling with God I never witnessed [before]. They prayed as though they saw their children and neighbors standing on the verge of destruction, and that, without an immediate interposition of almighty grace, they were lost forever."[22]

The founding, reestablishment, or intensified activity of such prayer meetings usually marked the early stages of the Presbyterian revivals of the Second Awakening. Their activity notified the congregation that it was not as pious as it had been or could be, and that reform was necessary. Much like jeremiads, lay prayers were both admissions of communal guilt and calls to self-examination and repentence. In the small towns of the early republic, the organization of such prayer groups did not go unnoticed. Knowing that the pious were praying for a revival and that their prayers were often efficacious, men and women involuntarily became more alert to the state of their souls. Anxiety grew and some of the more sensitive began to see spiritual admonitions in otherwise everyday events: a chance sermon on the need for conversion seemed a direct reproach; a sudden death in the community, a warning to repent. Undoubtedly, the pious accompanied their prayers with more informal attempts at arousing religious concern, such as direct inquiries after their neighbors' spiritual welfare. Through their prayers and actions, the devout confronted the community with its sinfulness and encouraged a resolve to repent.

In this regard Second Awakening revivals often began much as had Elizabethtown's 1771–72 revival. The lay role in the later revivals, however, differed in two respects. First, women were often the devout who formed prayer groups and thereby initiated reform. No Presbyterian revival account before 1800 mentions the role of women, but by the Second Awakening the rising power of the laity had expanded to include females.[23] Ministers shared evangelical responsibility with women as well as men. Secondly, by 1800 the male lay role had been institutionalized in the office of church elder. Although many Presbyterian congregations had elders before 1740, the office did not become a staple in church life until after the First Awakening.[24] It is difficult to determine what part elders played in the revivals between the Awakenings, but their activity in revivals after 1800 is prominent. Along with the devout women of the church, they played a crucial role in alerting the congregation to its low state of religion.

Since their main duties were the discipline of church morals and the examination of prospective members' piety, the elders were periodically confronted with direct evidence of the spiritual state of the church. Whether they responded to declension with positive actions depended on their own piety and dedication, as well as that of the minister who sat with them in session. Many sessions met infrequently, examined candidates perfunctorily, enforced church discipline rarely, and never participated in presbytery or synod, thus eliminating the importance of elders in church life. Other more conscientious and well-organized sessions played major roles in the origin and progress of revivals. Like the members of prayer meetings, elders occasionally met to discuss the virtue and piety of their community. For example, in 1807, when no one requested admission to the Connecticut Farms Presbyterian Church, the session agreed to spend its meeting in prayer for a revival.[25] And in 1829 the Oxford Presbyterian Church resolved that the elders spend an hour every Saturday night in self-examination and prayer because of the lack of piety in their community. They also agreed to meet once a month "for mutual conference and prayer for the outpouring of the Spirit upon our Congregation."[26]

Other sessions took more active measures to encourage piety in their congregations. The session of Newark First Church divided its congregation into districts and ordered its members to visit each family in their assigned neighborhoods and "converse with them on the subject of personal religion."[27] The prayers and visits of the elders emphasized the need for reform, while the systematic way in which the community was reached encouraged mass concern for religion.

The appointment—by session, synod, or presbytery—of a day of fasting, humiliation and prayer was crucial in both inspiring the pious to work for a revival and in spreading that religious concern to the congregation at large. Fast days were a common institution throughout the colonial era and the early national period; they were not used in Elizabethtown's 1771–72 revival, but were common in Second Awakening revivals. In a typical promulgation, Springfield Presbyterian Church made February 6, 1819, a day of fasting "considering the aspect of Providence towards us as a church and people, and remembering the coldness and [spiritual] stupidity which have so long prevailed."[28] Such days served much the same purpose as prayer meetings: they called attention to the congregation's sinful state and to the need for divine grace. But a fast day engaged the whole congregation rather than just a small part of it in spiritual self-examination. Often men and women set aside their work and spent the entire day in attention to religion. During part of the fast day the congregation usually prayed privately at home; often it also publicly assembled to hear a sermon demanding spiritual reformation and to pray that God would turn away His wrath and bless them with a revival. The fast day effectively separated men and women from the preoccupations of the world and confronted them with the need for salvation.

The Westfield revival of 1825 demonstrates the roles prayer, elders, and fast days played in promoting religious concern.[29] The Westfield session described the condition of the church by December 1824 as "truly appalling":

> A spiritual death had frozen the hearts of Professors. And as the natural consequence, the Congregation in general were negligent and indifferent about the spiritual interests of their souls. But while there were some few professors disheartened at these prospects and disposed to hang their harps upon the willows, and sit down and weep in despondency, the LORD had a blessing in reserve for the people.

At this point the Westfield Church held a fast day at the behest of the Synod of New Jersey. To the surprise of the elders a large number attended the day-long religious exercises. The prayers for a revival offered at these services deeply affected the elders and devout members of the church and convinced them of their own laxity:

> Many lost their hope of peace with GOD though they had long been members of unsuspected piety; and were deeply distressed with a conviction of their criminal declension in the work of GOD, and, as a just consequence, with the loss of the light of GOD's countenance. They determined to bear the indignation of the LORD, because they had sinned against him, until he should plead their cause and execute judgment for them. They still hoped confidently that the LORD would bring them forth to the light and that they should behold his righteousness.

Feeling the necessity of action, the session organized weekly prayer meetings, "spent in prayer and praise and free conversation on the state of personal piety." In a few weeks the elders established prayer societies throughout the congregation as well, and attended them in pairs "without the interference of the Pastor." By January 1825 people were beginning to inquire "what they should do to be saved." On the third Thursday of the month the session held another fast day, bringing together the families they had visited individually. "The religious exercises of that memorable day," the elders later reported, "were through the divine blessing made as the fire and the hammer that breaketh the rock in pieces." In short, a revival had begun in Westfield.

As the revival entered its second stage and sinners began to ask the way to Christ, the prayer meetings which had preceded the revival gained an additional function. Composed of the most faithful and devout church members, they were an excellent source of practical advice on conversion and the holy life. As prayers for a revival bore fruit, sinners flocked to these meetings. For example, in Newark First Church in 1816, where usually only twenty or thirty attended prayer societies, suddenly two hundred came to lament their sins and ask the way to salvation.[30] To accommodate such numbers, the church organized prayer groups in each neighborhood, dividing them according to sex, color, and, occasionally, age. Men and women and blacks and whites met separately, both satisfying the nineteenth century's sense of decorum and bringing together people of the same background so that they could identify with each other and share common experiences.

The Presbyterian Church recognized the importance of prayer meetings in both daily church life and revivals. Presbyterians encouraged churches to establish them, and ministers praised their part in fostering piety; in its description of the 1825 revival, the Westfield session singled out "private christians," "the pious," and the women of the church as having done the most in promoting that town's revival.[31] Lay meetings also had a stabilizing effect once revivals were in progress. In a small group of neighbors, emotionalism was less likely than in the anonymity of a large camp meeting. Moreover, the prayer group's continuous watch over sinners encouraged conversion to be a steady, gradual, and private process rather than an immediate and public one. If there was a danger in prayer meetings, it was censoriousness. The feelings of exultation and righteousness which had marred the First Awakening, however, seem to have been at a minimum in the Second.

How crucial these lay activities were to the revival depended on the degree of organization and dedication among elders and church members. Where they were weak or indifferent, or where the minister was unusually forceful, the laity's role was correspondingly reduced. But in most Second Awakening revivals before New Measures, devout church members and elders played a significant preparatory and advisory role.

This is not to say that the minister's role in the Second Awakening revival was negligible. With his elders the pastor periodically visited each prayer meeting to preach on experimental religion, thus discouraging departures from church dogma among the laity. The morning after a fast day, a minister often awoke to find dozens of men and women waiting to ask him what they could do to be saved. The Reverend Abel Jackson of Bloomfield reported that it was not uncommon for between fifty and one hundred to gather at his house for religious instruction during his 1800 revival.[32] The midweek lectures that were sparsely attended in nonrevival years were crowded during periods of religious concern. They gave the minister a chance to address those already under conviction as well as the merely curious, who frequently came as cynics but went away stricken sinners. At these lectures ministers often delivered impassioned sermons on the need for conversion, providing a dramatic counterpoint to methodical lay activities.

The dramatic element that the minister provided for the Second Awakening, however, was of a different sort than the one that had characterized the First Awakening. Most Presbyterian revivals of the early nineteenth century occurred under the preaching of the local pastor; few free-lance itinerants roamed the New Jersey countryside to intrude on other ministers' parishes. The Presbyterian Church did allow an itinerancy of a sort in the Second Awakening: the clerical preaching tour. This was used as early as 1803 in New Jersey's Second Awakening, and throughout this period presbyteries occasionally sent clergymen on circuit to promote religion.[33] Touring ministers usually traveled in pairs and spent a day or two in each town within their presbyteries, where they preached and organized religious meetings. They visited churches with pastors as well as ones without settled ministers and outposts of congregations whose inhabitants rarely attended church. These tours were an institutionalization of the itinerancy which had been so effective in spreading religious enthusiasm during the First Awakening, yet so disruptive to church order. They differed from the itinerancy of the 1740s in that ministers now went on tour at the direction of their presbytery rather than in response to their own inner gift or calling: order had replaced charisma, and divisiveness and emotionalism were thereby avoided without sacrificing the usefulness of itinerancy in spreading religion.

These preaching tours proved to be enormously useful in broadening the scope of the Second Awakening. Since they often began in an attempt to spread the revival spirit already present in one town, touring clergy delivered strongly evangelical sermons with the hope that the whole countryside would come alive with the desire to be saved. And, in fact, it often did. Under the combined influence of prayer meetings, fast days, and preaching tours, the revival spirit spread from the congregation to the entire community. As it did so, it touched men and women unaffiliated with the church where the revival had begun, and thereby transformed the communal order.

Catherine Elmer, the wife of a wealthy businessman in Westfield, breathlessly reported how the 1819 revival affected her town:

> Indeed you never saw such a time, I am sure I never did, to see the people flocking to church in crowds, three times on the Sabbath and every evening in the week in different neighborhoods, to see the Ministers so engaged. We have had four here in one day, and seven in a week—when [her daughter] Caroline had been home a fortnight, she had learned by heart 18 sermons and could remember every text.[34]

Mrs. Elmer's other daughter was less pleased with these developments; in a letter written at the beginning of the revival she complained that "there is nothing [to] talk about in Westfield but religion."[35] This was often the case during revivals, which usually occurred in the winter months, when there was little else to do. Between fall harvest and spring planting the revival often provided the only excitement in town. Prayer meetings and inquiry groups replaced the frolics and sewing bees that had flourished in the summer. A community's change from religious indifference to mass religious enthusiasm filled clergy and laity alike with awe and joy, prompting feelings similar to those of one observer of a Morristown revival: "Jehovah is marching through this town with majestic sway, rescuing rebels from the power of the prince of darkness, and frustrating his plans for their destruction."[36]

The Second Awakening was a victory for a new revival form as well as for Jehovah. Yet that victory was an ironic one. The techniques developed to produce a respectable and frequent revivalism caused problems of their own. In the first place, they reduced clerical authority. In contrast to the First Awakening, which had exalted the evangelist who could divine sinners' hearts, the Second Awakening diffused authority among ministers, elders, and the church's devout men and women. Presbyterian ministers never recovered that authority. Even when itinerant evangelists began to reappear in the 1820s, they shared the work of revival creation with the laity.

The Second Awakening's revival structure also created problems for Presbyterian theology. Orthodox Calvinism taught that God arbitrarily bestowed His grace on sinners without regard for their actions. The disposition to wait for a "divine downpour" during the First Awakening, rather than work for it, reflected the popular acceptance of this view. But by 1800 the very structure of revivals taught that God was responsive to human needs and implied He was controllable. The crucial role the laity played in fostering religious concern made grace seem less an arbitrary gift of God than the inevitable result of human effort. Clergymen cautioned church members to pray with a sense of dependence on God, but expectations that He would respond with a revival, and knowledge that revivals almost invariably followed lay efforts, made the whole procedure mechanical. It gave the impression that what people did was as important as what God did; indeed, it transformed God's actions into a mere extension of human behavior. The very form of Second Awakening revivals subtly encouraged Arminianism and helped fuel the theological controversies which wracked the Presbyterian Church during the nineteenth century.

Finally, American familiarity with this revival form affected the quality of religious enthusiasm itself. Unlike the situation during the First

Awakening—when the sheer novelty of mass religious emotion had encouraged disorder—the danger was that overfamiliarity would result in formalism, that the revival would become a religious rite the community was expected to undergo every few years as a matter of course. By the 1830s the revival seems to have become a familiar drama in which ministers, laity, and sinners knew their appropriate parts.

After the Second Awakening, the revival never lost its practiced air, despite periodic attempts to reinvigorate it. One such attempt, Charles Grandison Finney's New Measures, tried to put spontaneity back into the revival by intensifying the demand of the preacher upon his audience, quickening the pace of the revival, and making conversion an immediate and public act. Yet in practice the New Measures only continued the trends of the last century. Finney's revival techniques did not eliminate ritual; they only created a new type. Finney admitted as much in 1846.[37] His New Measures also continued the demystification of the revival: Finney's publication of a detailed revival manual in 1835 bared his revival machinery for all to see. And Finney depended on the laity as much as any small-town pastor for his evangelical efforts to succeed. Rather than changing the Second Awakening's revival form, New Measures epitomized it, for that form, in spreading evangelical responsibility from the ministry to the laity and in controlling the religious emotion which had disordered the First Awakening, assured the evangelical success which ministers had sought since the eighteenth century.

Notes

1. Calvin Colton, *History and Character of American Revivals of Religion* (London: F. Westley and A. H. Davis, 1832), p. 59.

2. The most prominent Presbyterian revival manuals of the early nineteenth century were Colton, *American Revivals of Religion*; William Buell Sprague, *Lectures on Revivals of Religion . . .*, 2nd ed. (New York: D. Appleton & Co., 1833); and Charles Grandison Finney, *Lectures on Revivals of Religion*, ed. William G. McLoughlin (Cambridge, Mass: Belknap Press of Harvard University Press, 1960). With the exception of Charles Roy Keller, historians of the Second Great Awakening have concentrated on the Southern camp meeting or Finney's New Measures and have neglected the small-town revivals which characterized the Awakening between about 1795 and 1825. On the local Congregationalist revivals of Connecticut, see Charles Roy Keller, *The Second Great Awakening in Connecticut*, Yale Historical Publications, Miscellany, 40 (New Haven: Yale University Press, London: Oxford University Press, 1942), chap. 3. On Finney's New Measures, see William G. McLoughlin, Jr., *Modern Revivalism: Charles Grandison Finney to Billy Graham* (New York: Ronald Press Co., 1959), chaps. 1–2, and Richard Carwardine, "The Second Great Awakening in the Urban Centers: An Examination of Methodists and the 'New Measures,' " *Journal of American History* 59 (1972): 327–340. On the frontier camp meeting, the most perceptive account is Dickson D. Bruce, Jr., *And They All Sang Hallelujah: Plain-Folk Camp-Meeting Religion, 1800–1845* (Knoxville: University of Tennessee Press, 1974).

3. Several accounts of New Jersey's First Awakening revivals have survived. Descriptions of the 1739–40 and 1741 Newark revivals and the 1740 Elizabethtown revival appear in the early American magazine, *The Christian History* 1 (1743): 252–58. John Rowland's 1739–40 revival is described in his "Narrative of the Revival and Progress of Religion, in the Towns of Hopewell, Amwell and Maiden-head, in New-Jersey, and New-Providence in Pennsylvania," which appears in Gilbert Tennent, *A Funeral Sermon Occasion'd by the Death of the Reverend Mr. John Rowland* . . . (Philadelphia: William Bradford, 1745), pp. 51–72. Greenwich's First Awakening revival is described in "Reports upon the Early History of Presbyterian Churches," *Journal of the Presbyterian Historical Society* 3 (1905): 87–88.

4. In 1740, for example, Blair, Finley, and Gilbert Tennent visited Deerfield among other places; see "Reports upon the Early History," p. 36.

5. Rowland, "Narrative of the Revival" p. 64; *The Christian History* 2 (1744): 246, 247; and the fifth, sixth and seventh journals in *George Whitefield's Journals* (1905; facsimile edition, Gainesville, Fla.: Scholars Facsimiles & Reprints, 1969), pp. 317–511.

6. In 1746 Jonathan Dickinson, Elizabethtown's New Side pastor, accurately observed that "there is no where to be found a Ministry more united in Sentiments than those of this Province." Dickinson to Thomas Foxcroft, Elizabethtown, Nov. 24, 1746, Thomas Foxcroft Correspondence, Princeton University Library, Princeton, N.J. Martin Lodge, in his detailed study of the First Awakening in the Middle Colonies, could find no evidence of lay exhortation, and few separations or defections to the Baptists occurred. See Martin Ellsworth Lodge, "The Great Awakening in the Middle Colonies" (Ph.D. diss., University of California, Berkeley, 1964), p. 261, and Norman Hall Maring, *Baptists in New Jersey: A Study in Transition* (Valley Forge: Judson Press, 1964), pp. 47–48.

7. Rowland, "Narrative of the Revival," pp. 53–54, 66.

8. *The Christian History* 2 (1744): 307.

9. "Sketch of the Life of Rev. Jacob Green, A.M.," *The Christian Advocate* 9 (1831): 634.

10. Tennent, *Funeral Sermon*, p. 6.

11. T[homas] Arthur, *A Sermon Preached at the Ordination of the Rev. Mr. Daniel Thane, at Connecticut-Farms, in New-Jersey, August 29th, 1750* . . . (New York: James Parker, 1750), p. 26.

12. *A Brief Account of the Life of the Late Rev. Caleb Smith* . . . (Woodbridge: J. Parker, 1763), p. 4.

13. Since there had been few separations or lay itinerants in New Jersey during the Awakening, Presbyterian ministers had little of the fear of lay evangelicalism so common to the New England clergy. Nor did they possess their Congregationalist colleagues' reluctance to share responsibilities with lay elders. The elder had always been an integral part of Presbyterian church government; in the pluralistic Middle Colonies the office recognized the very real power laity wielded in church affairs. Presbyterian polity, Middle Colony conditions, and the New Side's ideals and experience all encouraged New Jersey's ministers to both welcome and enlist lay evangelical efforts.

14. *The Christian History* 1 (1743): 253. Typically, when John Gano of New Jersey converted, he joined a group of young people in his neighborhood who met in the evening for prayer. See *Biographical Memoirs of the Late Rev. John Gano, of Frankfort, (Kentucky)* . . . (New York: Southwick and Hardcastle, 1806), pp. 20–21.

15. Colton, *American Revivals of Religion*, p. 82.

16. What we know of this revival is based upon a detailed description which a member of Elizabethtown's Presbyterian Church wrote in 1773; that a layman should write a revival account itself indicates the laity's rising importance in evangelical affairs. The revival account, dated Elizabeth-Town, April 28, 1773, and signed "J. L.," appears in Nicholas Murray, *Notes, Historical and Biographical, Concerning Elizabeth-Town: its Eminent Men, Churches and Ministers* (Elizabeth-Town, N.J.: E. Sanderson, 1844), pp. 137–51.

17. Although Elizabethtown's 1771–72 revival was a much more organized affair than any of the First Awakening's revivals and allowed laity a more important role, it was not totally divorced from the world of the 1740s. George Whitefield itinerated in New Jersey in 1770 and may well have provided an additional impetus to Elizabethtown's revival. J.

L.'s account does not mention Whitefield, but there is a good chance that in his last tour Whitefield visited Elizabethtown, the scene of his earliest triumph. See Whitefield to Robert Keen, June 14, 1770, Philadelphia, in Luke Tyerman, *The Life of the Rev. George Whitefield,* 2d ed. (London: Hodder and Stoughton, 1890), 2:589.

18. Colton, *American Revivals of Religion*, pp. 2, 4.

19. A pattern of sporadic local revivals characterized New Jersey Presbyterian churches during this period, with some churches experiencing them on an average of once every nine years.

20. Murray, *Notes, Historical and Biographical*, p. 152.

21. This phrase was used in Westfield session's description of its 1825 revival; see Records, 10 November 1825, Westfield Presbyterian Church, microfilm, Rutgers University Special Collections, New Brunswick, New Jersey (hereafter film, RUSC).

22. Asa Hillyer to an anonymous minister, n.d., but written about the 1807 revival, quoted in James Hoyt, *"The Mountain Society:" A History of the First Presbyterian Church, Orange, N.J.* (New York: C. M. Saxton, Barker & Co., 1860), p. 168. The role and attitudes of lay prayer meetings in revivals are also well described in the letter of Abel Jackson in *The New-York Missionary Magazine* . . . 3 (1802): 34–35 and in "Extract" in *The Religious Intelligencer*, 1, no. 42 (1817): 671–72.

23. During the Second Awakening in New Jersey, women not only conducted private prayer meetings but publicly exhorted sinners to repent with a fervor and ability that amazed Isaac Martin, a Rahway Friend long familiar with female "Public Friends." He observed that in Springfield's 1816 revival a dozen devout Presbyterian women "frequently visit families and exhort them, as they see occasion, or pray among them." See Isaac Martin, *A Journal of the Life, Travels, Labours, and Religious Exercises of Isaac Martin* . . . (Philadelphia: W. P. Gibbons 1834), p. 123.

24. Historians have yet to give the office of church elder the attention it deserves. A brief treatment of the subject appears in Guy Soulliard Klett, *Presbyterians in Colonial Pennsylvania* (Philadelphia: University of Pennsylvania Press; London, Oxford University Press, 1937), pp. 93, 199; and in Leonard J. Trinterud, *The Forming of an American Tradition: A Re-examination of Colonial Presbyterianism* (Philadelphia: Westminster Press, 1949), p. 274.

25. Records, 22 August 1807 (p. 33), First Presbyterian Church, Connecticut Farms, N.J., Connecticut Farms Presbyterian Church, Union, New Jersey. See also Records, 25 December 1816 (pp. 34–35), Bound Brook Presbyterian Church, film, RUSC.

26. Records, 17 February 1829 (pp. 24–25), Oxford Presbyterian Church, film, RUSC.

27. Records, 28 November 1828 (p. 81), First Presbyterian Church, Newark, New Jersey, Presbyterian Historical Society, Philadelphia (hereafter PHS).

28. Records, 1819 January 29 (p. 49), First Presbyterian Church, Springfield, New Jersey, PHS. See also August 15, 1816, *History of the First Presbyterian Church, Morristown, N.J.*, 2 vols. in 1 (Morristown: Banner Steam Printing, 1880?–91?), part 1, *Records of the Trustees and Session, 1742–1882*, p. 40; and Records, 23 August 1821 (p. 265), First Presbyterian Church, Elizabeth, New Jersey, PHS.

29. The following account of Westfield's 1825 revival is based on Records, 10 November 1825, Westfield Presbyterian Church, film, RUSC. The session believed that "the general features of this work of grace divine resembled most other revivals which bless the day in which we live."

30. "Revival of Religion [in Newark, 1816–17]," *The Religious Intelligencer* 1 (1817): 671.

31. Records, 10 November 1825, Westfield Presbyterian Church, film, RUSC.

32. Abel Jackson, letter, p. 34.

33. The role of the preaching tour in Second Awakening revivals is especially well described in "Revival of Religion in the Congregation of Basking Ridge, N.J.," in *The Religious Intelligencer* 7 (1823): 552–54.

34. Catherine Elmer to Betsey Elmer, 18 January 1819, folder 2, Elmer Family Papers, RUSC.

35. Nancy Elmer to her sisters, n.d., but almost certainly 1819, folder 3, Elmer Family Papers, RUSC.

36. Letter dated Morristown, May 12, 1822, *The Religious Remembrancer* no. 42, 9th series (1822): 167.
37. Finney, *Lectures on Revivals of Religion*, p. xlix.

Comments

Paul Johnson

Paul Johnson is a lecturer in history at Princeton University. In 1980 his *Shopkeeper's Millenium: Society and Revivals in Rochester, New York, 1815–1837* shared the Merle Curti Award for the best book in United States social history. He is working on a life of the nineteenth-century daredevil, Sam Patch.

THESE ESSAYS address the quality and consequences of evangelical spirituality in New Jersey from the Great Awakening through the early nineteenth century. Both are thoughtful, well researched, and on the whole convincing. But they do have problems. Milton J Coalter provides a detailed description of an important episode in the intellectual development of Gilbert Tennent, but generalizes only at a low level. Martha T. Blauvelt's essay is more imaginative, but she shares with Professor Coalter a problem that is common to any study of popular religion in the eighteenth-century Mid-Atlantic: we know too little about social history in that region to permit meaningful speculation about the contexts and results of New Jersey's religious revivals.

That is a severe limitation, but Coalter shows us that valuable things can be done within it. He carefully documents Gilbert Tennent's extensive borrowings from Dutch Pietism, particularly its insistence on personal conversion. From Theodorus Frelinghuysen, Tennent learned that preachers must terrify their hearers, break their pride, and render them aware of their absolute helplessness. That requires powerful preaching from a minister who has experienced conversion himself. (A revival minister, after all, is a guide to individual spiritual experience, and most of us prefer guides who have been where we are going.) Thinking and preaching along these lines, Tennent attacked cold ministers and formal religion in the name of vital piety, and that, of course, got him into trouble. Settled ministers recognized him as a dangerous agitator and reminded him that criticism of unregenerate ministers implied a kind of knowledge not available to any Calvinist who stands this side of the grave.

Professor Coalter shows us that that happened in the life of Gilbert Tennent, and that in the beginning much of it stemmed from the influence of Frelinghuysen. But he does not address the larger fact that Tennent's new practices and the forms of opposition they aroused were common to eighteenth-century revivals within Calvinism wherever they occurred. Revivalists always insisted on personal conversion, and often accompanied that insistence with attacks upon unconverted clergymen. Old-side ministers responded in kind, and much of the antirevival literature attacks evangelists as much for bad manners as for theological deviation. Thus while Coalter provides a thorough description of that theological and methodological episode as it was acted out in the career of Gilbert Tennent, we cannot be certain that Tennent would not have had a similar career or that New Jersey would not have had a similar Great Awakening had the young preacher never encountered Dutch Pietism. Indeed the paper demonstrates that after Tennent aroused opposition among his fellow Presbyterians he beat a successful tactical retreat and revised his thinking in ways that were acceptable to his denomination, and thus gained support and continued to be a leader. We leave the paper knowing that Frelinghuysen played a role in the intellectual development of Gilbert Tennent. But I am not convinced that Dutch Pietism was necessary either to him or to the Great Awakening among New Jersey Presbyterians.

Martha Blauvelt's broad and imaginative essay also begins with the fact that Awakeners spent their time converting sinners and not preaching received rules, then goes on to demonstrate the creation and institutionalization of revival forms. Churches organized themselves in ways that induced individual religious experience, and over the course of the seventy or so years following the Great Awakening the result was a transformation of authority within congregations. Both the constituted lay elders and ad hoc prayer groups of women and men gained power—power that they had created for themselves. Individual conversion remained the goal of the religious life, and the churches invented new forms and rituals through which the whole congregation cooperated in creating conversions. The result was twofold. First, individual spiritual transformation became predictable and ritualized (by the end of the paper, the nineteenth-century "machinery of revivals" is just around the corner); second, lay people assumed and then formalized their authority within the church.

It is an ingenious and convincing argument, but it does leave a few questions. First, Blauvelt argues that these were local revivals that posed no threat to settled ministers. But while there were no itinerants stealing prestige from local clergymen, it is clear that ministers were relinquishing important kinds of authority to lay people within their own congregations. Ministerial authority, as Blauvelt makes abundantly clear, was not what it had been before the revivals started. Second, most of these innovations took place between the Great Awakening and 1800. We know little about New Jersey revivals, but there is reason to suspect that these were relatively quiet years—a long cold spell punctuated by isolated local revivals. While Blauvelt finds new forms being created in those incidents, it is likely that converted Christians formed a smaller proportion of the population of New Jersey at the end of her period than at the beginning. Had Professor Blauvelt taken account of that, she might have presented her evidence in different ways.

Which brings up the central problem with both papers: their failure to transcend the narrow boundaries of religious history. Both assert that eighteenth-century revivals were based in individual spirituality. It follows that revival theology and revival techniques were devised with an audience in mind. Indeed it was the laity as much as the clergy that rejected received forms in favor of inner experience, and the question that must be asked (or at least recognized as a question) is, why did New Jersey Presbyterians make that rejection in the 1730s and 1740s? A second, closely related question is this: how did theological and organizational change relate to changes in society at large? Was the transformation of religion bound up with a larger social transformation? Was the contest over religious authority part of a larger contest?

Neither Coalter nor Blauvelt attempts to answer such questions, and for good reason: we know little about the social history of New Jersey. Students of the Great Awakening in New England, for instance, can (and therefore must) place their findings within a social, cultural, and political terrain that has been carefully reconstructed by a generation of busy scholars. Students of revivals in the Chesapeake can do the same. But social historians have stayed away from New Jersey, and for that reason students of New Jersey revivals can talk only about religion. The explanation, I suspect, is that social historians are afraid of the diversity of the Middle Colonies. The presence of a renowned Dutch Reformed theologian alongside a famed Presbyterian preacher in the little village of New Brunswick, for instance, is something that students of homogeneous New England or neatly divided Virginia and Maryland simply cannot tolerate. Historians of society like to do case studies, and they like to assume that "their" cases are meaningful outside the boundaries of single small towns. But eighteenth-century New Jersey was far too diverse to support such assumptions. Largely for that reason, social historians have been frightened away. And it is primarily because of that avoidance that work that would enable us to understand what New Jersey revivals were all about is a long way from being done.